The Art of Poetry, Vol

CCEA POETRY ANTHOLOGY

With thanks for their contributions to Carol Atherton, James Browning, Matthew Curry, Karen Elson, Johanna Harrison, Michael Meally and Sally Rowley.

Published by Peripeteia Press Ltd.

First published November 2017

ISBN: 978-1-9997376-8-9

Poetry is simply the most beautiful, impressive, and widely effective mode of saying things.

Matthew Arnold

Contents

Introduction

The philosopher Nietzsche described his work as 'the greatest gift that [mankind] has ever been given'. The Elizabethan poet Edmund Spenser hoped his epic, The Faerie Queene, would magically transform its readers into noblemen. In comparison, our aims for The Art of Poetry series of books are a little more modest. Fundamentally we aim to provide books that will be of maximum use to English students and their teachers. In our experience, few students read essays on poems, yet, whatever specification they are studying, they have to write analytical essays on poetry. So, we've offering some models, written in a lively, accessible and, we hope, engaging style. We believe that the essay as a form needs demonstrating and championing, especially as so many revision books for students present information in broken down note form.

For Volume 1 we chose canonical poems for several reasons: Firstly, they are simply great poems, well worth reading and studying; secondly, we chose poems from across time so that they sketch in outline major developments in English poetry, from the Elizabethan period up until the present day, so that the volume works as an introduction to poetry and poetry criticism. Our popular volumes 2-5 focused on poems set at A-level by the Edexcel and AQA boards respectively. Volumes 6 to 13 tackled GCSE and IGCSE anthologies from AQA, Eduqas, OCR and Edexcel. In this current volume, we our focus turns for the first time to CCEA, providing critical support for students reading poems from CCEA's latest GCSE poetry anthology. In particular, we hope our critical guide will be of help and will inspire those students who are aiming to reach the very highest grades.

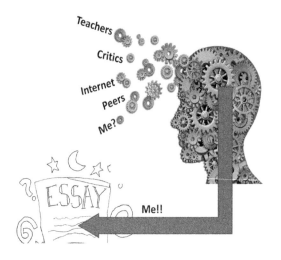

How to analyse a poem [seen or unseen]

A list of ingredients, not a recipe

Firstly, what not to do: sometimes pupils have been so programmed to spot poetic features such as alliteration that they start analysis of a poem with close reading of these micro aspects of technique. This is never a clever idea. A far better strategy is to begin by trying to develop an overall understanding of what you think the poem is about. While, obviously, all these poems are about relationships of some sort or other, the nature of these relationships vary widely what they have say about this topic is also highly varied. Once you've established the central concerns, you can delve into the poem's interior, examining its inner workings in the light of these. And you should be flexible enough to adapt, refine or even reject your initial thoughts in the light of your investigation. The essential thing is to make sure that whether you're discussing imagery or stanza form, sonic effects or syntax, enjambment or vocabulary, you always explore the significance of the feature in terms of meanings and effect.

Someone once compared texts to cakes. When you're presented with a cake the first thing you notice is what it looks like. Probably the next thing you'll do is taste it and find out if you like the flavour. This aesthetic experience will come first. Only later might you investigate the ingredients and how it was made. Adopting a uniform reading strategy is like a recipe; it sets out what you must, do step by step, in a predetermined order. This can be helpful, especially when you start reading and analysing poems. Hence in our first volume in The Art of Poetry series we explored each poem under the same subheadings of narrator, characters, imagery, patterns of sound, form & structure and contexts, and all our essays followed essentially the same direction. Of course, this is a reasonable strategy for reading poetry and will stand you in good stead. However, this present volume takes a different, more flexible approach, because this book is designed for students aiming for levels 7 to 9, or A to A* in old currency, and to reach the highest levels your work needs to be a bit more conceptual, critical and individual. Writing frames are useful for beginners, like stabilisers when you learn to ride a bike. But, if you wish to write top level essays you need to develop your own frames.

Read our essays and you'll find that they all include the same principle ingredients – detailed, 'fine-grained' reading of crucial elements of poetry, imagery, form, rhyme and so forth - but each essay starts in a different way and each one has a slightly different focus or weight of attention on the various aspects that make up a poem. Once you feel you have mastered the apprentice strategy of reading all poems in the same way, we strongly recommend you put this generic essay recipe approach to one side and move on to a new way of reading, an approach that can change depending on the nature of the poem you're reading.

Follow your nose

Having established what you think a poem is about - its theme and what is interesting about the poet's treatment of the theme [the conceptual bit] - rather than then working through a pre-set agenda, decide what you honestly think are the most interesting aspects of the poem and start analysing these closely. This way your response will be original [a key marker of a top band essay] and you'll be writing about material you find most interesting. In other words, you're foregrounding yourself as an individual, critical reader. These most interesting aspects might be ideas or technique based, or both.

Follow your own, informed instincts, trust in your own critical intelligence as a reader. If you're writing about material that genuinely interests you, your writing is likely to be interesting for the examiner too. And, obviously, take advice to from your teacher too, use their expertise.

Because of the focus on sonic effects and imagery other aspects of poems are often overlooked by students. It is a rare student, for instance, who notices how punctuation works in a poem and who can write about it convincingly. Few students write about the contribution of the unshowy function words, such as pronouns, prepositions or conjunctions, yet these words are crucial to any text. Of course, it would be a highly risky strategy to focus your whole essay on a seemingly innocuous and incidental detail of a poem. But coming at things from an unusual angle is as important to writing great essays as it is to the production of great poetry.

So, in summary, when reading a poem for the first time, such as when doing an 'unseen' style question, have a check list in mind, but don't feel you must follow someone else's generic essay recipe. Don't feel that you must always start with a consideration of imagery if the poem you're analysing has, for instance, an eye-catching form. Consider the significance of major features, such as imagery, vocabulary, sonic patterns and form. Try to write about these aspects in terms of their contribution to themes and effects. But also follow your nose, find your own direction, seek out aspects that genuinely engage you and write about these.

The essays in this volume provide examples and we hope they will encourage you to go your own way, at least to some extent, and to make discoveries for yourself. No single essay could possibly cover everything that could be said about any one of these poems; aiming to create comprehensive essays like this would be utterly foolish. And we have not tried to do so. Nor are our essays meant to be models for exam essays – they're far too long for that. They do, however, illustrate the sort of conceptualised, critical and 'fine-grained' exploration demanded for top grades at GCSE and beyond. There's always more to be discovered, more to say, space in other words for you to develop some original reading of your own, space for you to write your own individual essay recipe.

Writing Literature essays

The Big picture and the small

An essay itself can be a form of art. And writing a great essay takes time, skill and practice. And also expert advice. Study the two figures in the picture carefully and describe what you can see. Channel your inner Sherlock Holmes to add any deductions you are able to form about the image. Before reading what we have to say, write your description out as a prose paragraph. Probably you'll have written something along the following lines:

First off, the overall impression: this picture is very blurry. Probably this indicates that either this is a very poor quality reproduction, or that it is a copy of a very small detail from a much bigger image that has been magnified several times. The image shows a stocky man and a medium-sized dog, both orientated towards something to their left, which suggests there is some point of interest in that direction. From the man's rustic dress [smock, breeches, clog-like boots] the picture is either an old one or a modern one depicting the past. The man appears to be carrying a stick and there's maybe a bag on his back. From all of these details we can probably deduce that he's a peasant, maybe a farmer or a shepherd.

 Now do the same thing for picture two. We have even less detail here and again the picture's blurry. Particularly without the benefit of colour it's hard to determine what

we're seeing other than a horizon and maybe the sky. We might just be able to make out that in the centre of the picture is the shape of the sun. From the reflection, we can deduce that the image is of the sun either setting or rising over water. If it is dawn this usually symbolises hope, birth and new beginnings; if the sun is setting it conventionally symbolises the opposite – the end of things, the coming of night/ darkness, death.

If you're a sophisticated reader, you might well start to think about links between the two images. Are they, perhaps, both details from the same single larger image, for instance.

Well, this image might be even harder to work out. Now we don't even have

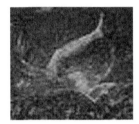

a whole figure, just a leg, maybe, sticking up in the air. Whatever is happening here, it looks painful and we can't even see the top half of the body. From the upside orientation, we might guess that the figure is or has fallen. If we put this image with the one above, we might think the figure has fallen into water as there are horizontal marks on the image that could be splashes. From the quality of this image we can deduce that this is an even smaller detail blown-up.

You may be wondering by now why we've suddenly moved into rudimentary art appreciation. On the other hand, you may already have worked out the point of this exercise. Either way, bear with us, because this is the last picture for you to describe and analyse. So, what have we here? Looks like another peasant, again from the past, perhaps medieval [?] from the smock-like dress, clog-like shoes and the britches. This character is also probably male and seems to be pushing some wooden apparatus from left to right. From the ridges at the bottom left of the image we can surmise that he's working the land, probably driving a plough. Noticeably the figure has his back to us; we see his turned away from us, suggesting his whole concentration is on the task at hand. In the background appear to be sheep, which would fit with our impression that this is an image of farming. It seems likely that this image and the first one come from the same painting. They have a similar style and subject and it is possible that these sheep belong to our first character. This image is far less blurry than the other one. Either it is a better-quality reproduction, or this is a larger, more significant detail extracted from the original source. If this is a significant detail it's interesting that we cannot see the character's face. From this we can deduce that he's not important in and of himself; rather he's a representative figure and the important thing is what he is and what he isn't looking at.

Okay, we hope we haven't stretched your patience too far. What's the point of all this? Well, let's imagine we prefixed the paragraphs above with an introduction, along the following lines: 'The painter makes this picture interesting and powerful by using several key techniques and details' and that we added a conclusion, along the lines of 'So now I have shown how the painter has made this picture interesting and powerful through the use of a number of key techniques and details'. Finally, substitute painter and picture for writer and text. If we put together our paragraphs into an essay what would be its strengths and weaknesses? What might be a better way of writing our essay?

Consider the strengths first off. The best bits of our essay, we humbly suggest, are the bits where we begin to explain what we are seeing, when we do the Holmes like deductive thinking. Another strength might be that we have started to make links between the various images, or parts of a larger image, to see how they work together to provide us more information. A corresponding weakness is that each of our paragraphs seems like a separate chunk of writing. The weaker parts of the paragraphs are where we simply describe what we can see. More importantly though, if we used our comments on image one as our first paragraph we seem to have started in a rather random way. Why should we have begun our essay with that image? What was the logic behind that? And most importantly of all, if this image is an analogue for a specific aspect of a text, such as a poem's imagery or a novel's dialogue we have dived straight into to analysing this technical aspect before we're established any overall sense of the painting/ text. And this is a very common fault with GCSE English Literature essays. As we've said before and will keep saying, pupils start writing detailed micro-analysis of a detail such as alliteration before they have established the big picture of what the text is about and what the answer to the question they've been set might be. Without this big picture it's very difficult to write about the significance of the micro details. And the major marks for English essays are reserved for explanations of the significance and effects generated by a writer's craft.

Now we'll try a different and much better approach. Let's start off with the big picture, the whole image. The painting on the next page is called *Landscape with the fall of Icarus*. It's usually attributed to the Renaissance artist, Pieter Breughel and was probably painted in the 1560s. Icarus is a character from Greek mythology. He was the son of the brilliant inventor, Daedalus. Trapped on Crete by the evil King Minos, Daedalus and Icarus managed to escape when the inventor created pairs of giant feathered wings. Before they took to sky Daedalus warned his son not to get too excited and fly too near the sun as the wings were held together by wax that might melt. Icarus didn't listen, however. The eventual result was that he plummeted back to earth, into the sea more precisely and was killed.

Applying this contextual knowledge to the painting we can see that the image is about how marginal Icarus' tragedy is in the big picture. Conventionally we'd expect any image depicting such a famous myth to make Icarus's fall the dramatic centre of attention. The main objects of this painting, however, are emphatically not the falling boy hitting the water. Instead our eye is drawn to the peasant in the centre of the painting, pushing his plough [even more so in colour as his shirt is the only red object in an otherwise greeny-yellow landscape] and the stately galleon sailing calmly past those protruding legs. Seeing the whole image, we can appreciate the significance of the shepherd and the ploughman looking up and down and to the left. The point being made is how they don't even notice the tragedy because they have work to do and need to get on with their lives. The animals too seem unconcerned. As W. H. Auden puts it, in lines from *Musée des Beaux Arts*, 'everything turns away / Quite leisurely from the disaster'.

To sum up, when writing an essay on any literary text do not begin with close-up analysis of micro-details. Begin instead with establishing the whole picture: What the text is about, what key techniques the writer uses, when it was written, what sort of text it is, what effects it has on the reader. Then, when you zoom in to examine smaller details, such as imagery, individual words, metre or sonic techniques you can discuss these in relation to their significance in terms of this bigger picture.

What would our art appreciation essay look like now?

Paragraph #1: Introduction – myth of Icarus, date of painting, the way our eyes is drawn away from his tragic death to much more ordinary life going around him. Significance of this – even tragic suffering goes on around us without us even noticing, we're too busy getting on with our lives.

Paragraph #2: We could, of course, start with our first figure and follow the same order as we've presented the images here. But wouldn't it make more logical sense to discuss first the biggest, more prominent images in the painting first? So, our first paragraph is about the ploughman and his horse. How his figure placed centrally and is bent downwards towards the ground and turned left away from us etc.

Paragraph #3: The next most prominent image is the ship. Also moving from right to left, as if the main point of interest in the painting is off in that direction. Here we could consider the other human agricultural figure, the shepherd and his dog and, of course, the equally oblivious sheep.

Paragraph #4: Having moved on to examining background details in the painting we could discuss the symbolism of the sun on the horizon. While this could be the sun rising, the context of the story suggests it is more likely to be setting. The pun of the sun/son going down makes sense.

Paragraph #5: Finally, we can turn our attention to the major historical and literary figure in this painting, Icarus and how he is presented. This is the key image in terms of understanding the painting's purpose and effect.

Paragraph #6: Conclusion. What is surprising about this picture. How do the choices the painter makes affect us as viewer/ reader? Does this painting make Icarus's story seem more pathetic, more tragic or something else?

Now, all you have to do is switch from a painting to a poem.

Big pictures, big cakes, recipes and lists of instructions; following your own nose and going your own way. Whatever metaphors we use, your task is to bring something personal and individual to your critical reading of poems and to your essay writing.

Writing comparative essays

The following is adapted from our discussion of this topic in *The Art of Writing English Literature Essays A-level* course companion, and is a briefer version, tailored to the GCSE exam task. Fundamentally comparative essays want you to display not only your ability to intelligently talk about literary texts, but also your ability to make meaningful connections between them. The first starting point is your topic. This must be broad enough to allow substantial thematic overlapping of the texts. However, too little overlap and it will be difficult to connect the texts; too much overlap and your discussion will be lopsided and one-dimensional. In the case of the CCEA GCSE, the exam question will ask you to focus on the methods used by the poets to explore how two poems present one of the three themes. You will also be directed to write specifically on language and imagery [AO2].

You will have the choice of two questions on each themed cluster [identity, relationships and conflct] from the poetry anthology. One named poem will be chosen for you and you will then have to choose an appropriate companion poem. Selecting the right poem for interesting comparison is obviously very important. Obviously, you should prepare for this question beforehand by pairing up the poems, especially as you will only have one hour to complete this task.

To think about this task visually, you don't want Option A, below, [not enough overlap] or Option B [two much overlap]. You want Option C. This option allows substantial common links to be built between your chosen texts where discussion arises from both fundamental similarities AND differences.

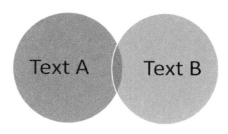

Option A: too many differences

Option B: too many similarities

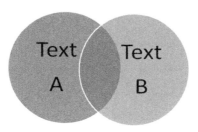

Option C: suitable number of similarities and differences

The final option will generate the most interesting discussion as it will allow substantial similarities to emerge as well as differences. The best comparative essays actually find that what seemed like clear similarities become subtle differences and vice versa while still managing to find rock solid similarities to build their foundations on.

Check the mark scheme for this question and you'll notice that to reach the top grade your comparison must be 'well-structured'. How should you structure a comparative essay? Consider the following alternatives. Which one is best and why?

Essay Structure #1

1. Introduction

2. Main body paragraph #1 - Text A

3. Main body paragraph #2 - Text A

4. Main body paragraph #3 - Text B

5. Main body paragraph #4 - Text B

6. Conclusion

Essay Structure #2

1. Introduction

2. Main body paragraph #1 - Text A

3. Main body paragraph #2 - Text A

4. Main body paragraph #3 - Text B

5. Main body paragraph #4 - Text B

6. Comparison of main body paragraphs #1 & #3 - Text A + B

7. Comparison of main body paragraphs #2 & #4 - Text A + B

8. Conclusion

Essay Structure #3

1. Introduction

2. Main body paragraph #1 - Text A + B

3. Main body paragraph #2 - Text A + B

4. Main body paragraph #3 - Text A + B

5. Main body paragraph #4 - Text A+ B

6. Conclusion

We hope you will agree that 3 is the optimum option. Option 1 is the dreaded 'here is everything I know about text A, followed by everything I know by Text B' approach where the examiner has to work out what the connections are between the texts. This will score the lowest marks. Option 2 is better: There is some attempt to compare the two texts. However, it is a very inefficient way of comparing the two texts. For comparative essay writing the most important thing is to discuss both texts together. This is the most effective and efficient way of achieving your overall aim. Option 3 does this by comparing and contrasting the two texts under common umbrella headings. This naturally encourages comparison. Using comparative discourse markers, such as 'similarly', 'in contrast to', 'conversely' 'likewise' and 'however' also facilitates effective comparison.

When writing about each poem, make sure you do not work chronologically through a poem, summarising the content of each stanza. Responses of this sort typically start with 'In the first stanza' and employ discourse markers of time rather than comparison, such as 'after', 'next', 'then' and so forth. Even if your reading is analytical rather than summative, your essay should not work through the poem from the opening to the ending. Instead, make sure you write about the ideas explored in both texts [themes], the feelings and effects generated and the techniques the poets utilise to achieve these.

Writing about language

Poems are paintings as well as windows; we look at them as well as through them. As you know, special attention should be paid to language in poetry because of all the literary art forms poetry, in particular, employs language in a precise, self-conscious and distinctive way. Ideally in poetry, every word should count. Analysis of language falls into distinct categories:

- By diction we mean the vocabulary used in a poem. A poem might be composed from the ordinary language of everyday speech or it might use elaborate, technical or elevated phrasing. Or both. At one time, some words and types of words were considered inappropriate for the rarefied field of poetry. The great Irish poet, W. B. Yeats never referred to modern technology in his poetry, there are no cars, or tractors or telephones, because he did not consider such things fitting for poetry. When much later, Philip Larkin used swear words in his otherwise well-mannered verse the effect was deeply shocking. Modern poets have pretty much dispensed with the idea of there being an elevated literary language appropriate for poetry. Hence in the CCEA anthology you'll find all sorts of modern, everyday language.

- Grammatically a poem may use complex or simple sentences [the key to which is the conjunctions]; it might employ a wash of adjectives and adverbs, or it may rely extensively on the bare force of nouns and verbs. Picking out and exploring words from specific grammatical classes has the merit of being both incisive and usually illuminating.

- Poets might mix together different types, conventions and registers of language, moving, for example, between formal and informal, spoken and written, modern and archaic, and so forth. Arranging the diction in the poem in terms of lexico-semantic fields, by register or by etymology, helps reveal underlying patterns of meaning.

- For almost all poems imagery is a crucial aspect of language. Broadly imagery is a synonym for description and can be broken down into two types, sensory and figurative. Sensory imagery means the words and phrases that appeal to our senses, to touch and taste, hearing, smell and sight. Sensory imagery is evocative; it helps to take us into the world of the poem to share the experience being described. Figurative imagery, in particular, is always significant. As we have mentioned, not all poems rely on metaphors and similes; these devices are only part of a poet's box of tricks, but figurative language is always important when it occurs because it compresses multiple meanings into itself. To use a technical term figurative images are polysemic - they contain many meanings. Try writing out the all the meanings contained in a metaphor in a more concise and economical way. Even simple, everyday metaphors compress meaning. If we want to say our teacher is fierce and powerful and that we fear his or her wrath, we can more concisely say our teacher is a dragon.

Writing about patterns of sound

Like painters, some poets have powerful visual imaginations, while other poets have stronger auditory imaginations are more like musicians. And some poems are like paintings, others are more like pieces of music.

Firstly, what not to do: Tempting as it may be to spot sonic features of a poem and list these, don't do this. Avoid something along the lines of 'The poet uses alliteration here and the rhyme scheme is ABABCDCDEFEFGG'. Sometimes, indeed, it may be tempting to set out the poem's whole rhyme scheme like this. Resist the temptation: This sort of identification of features is worth zero marks. Marks in exams are reserved for attempts to link techniques to meanings and to effects.

Probably many of us have been sitting in English lessons listening somewhat sceptically as our English teacher explains the surprisingly specific significance of a seemingly random piece of alliteration in a poem. Something along the lines 'The double d sounds here reinforce a sense of invincible strength' or 'the harsh repetition of the 't' sounds suggests anger'. Through all our minds at some point may have passed the idea that, in these instances, English teachers appear to be using some sort of Enigma-style secret symbolic decoding machine that reveals how particular patterns of sounds have such definite encoded meanings.

And this sort of thing is not all nonsense. Originally deriving from an oral tradition, poems are, of course, written for the ear as much as for the eye, to be heard as much as read. A poem is a soundscape as much as it is a set of meanings. Sounds are, however, difficult to tie to very definite meanings and effects. By way of example, the old BBC Radiophonic workshop, which produced ambient sounds for radio and television programmes, used the same sounds in different contexts, knowing that the audience would perceive them in the appropriate way because of that context. Hence the sound of bacon sizzling, of an audience clapping and of feet walking over gravel were actually recordings of an identical sound.

Listeners heard them differently because of the context. So, we may, indeed, be able to spot the repeated 's' sounds in a poem, but whether this creates a hissing sound, yes like a snake, or the susurration of the sea will depend on the context within the poem and the ears of the 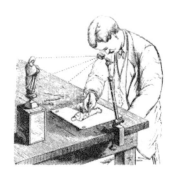 reader. Whether a sound is soft and soothing or harsh and grating is also open to interpretation.

The idea of connecting these sounds to meanings or significance is a productive one. And your analysis will be most convincing if you use several pieces of evidence together. In other words, rather than try to pick out individual examples of sonic effects we recommend you explore the weave or pattern of sounds, the effects these generate and their contribution to feelings and ideas. For example, this might mean examining how alliteration and assonance are used together to achieve a particular mimetic effect.

Writing about form & structure

As you know, there are no marks for simply identifying textual features. This holds true for language, sounds and also for form. Consider instead the relationship between a poem's form and its content, themes and effects. Form is not merely decorative or ornamental: A poem's meanings and effects are generated through the interplay of form and content. Broadly speaking the form can either work with or against a poem's content. Conventionally a sonnet, for instance, is about love, whereas a limerick is a comic form. A serious love poem in the form of a limerick would be unusual, as would a sonnet about an old man with a beard.

Sometimes poetic form can create an ironic backdrop to highlight an aspect of content. An example would be a formally elegant poem about something

monstrous, or a fragile form containing something robust or vice versa. Browning's *The Laboratory* might spring to mind. The artist Grayson Perry uses form in this ironic way. Rather than depicting the sort of picturesque, idealised images we expect of ceramics, Perry's pots and urns depict modern life in bright, garish colours. The urn pictured, for instance, is entitled Modern Family and depicts two gay men with a boy who they have presumably adopted. A thrash metal concert inside a church, a philosophical essay via text message, a fine crystal goblet filled with cherryade would be further examples of ironic relationships between message and medium, content and context or form.

****

Reading form

Put a poem before your eyes. Start off taking a panoramic perspective: Think of the forest, not the trees. Perhaps mist over your eyes a bit. Don't even read the words, just look at the poem, like at a painting. Is the poem slight, thin, fat, long, short? What is the relation of whiteness to blackness? Why might the poet have chosen this shape? Does it look regular or irregular? A poem about a long winding river will probably look rather different from one about a small pebble, or should do. Unless form is being employed ironically. Now read the poem a couple of times. First time, fast as you can, second time more slowly and carefully. How does the visual layout of the poem relate to what it seems to be about? Does this form support, or create a tension against, the content? Is the form one you recognise, like a sonnet, or is it more open, more irregular like free verse? Usually the latter is obvious from the irregularity of the stanzas, line lengths and lack of metre or rhyme.

As Hurley and O'Neill explain in Poetic Form: An Introduction, like genre, form sets expectations: 'In choosing form, poets bring into play associations and expectations which they may then satisfy, modify or subvert'.[1] We've already suggested that if we see a poem is a sonnet or a limerick this recognition will set up expectations about the nature of the poem's content. The same thing works on a smaller level; once we have noticed that a poem's first stanza is a quatrain, we expect it to continue in this neat, orderly fashion. If the quatrain's rhyme scheme is xaxa, xbxb, in which only the second and fourth lines rhyme, we reasonably expect that the next stanza will be xcxc. So, if it isn't we need to consider why.

---

[1] Hurley & O'Neill, *Poetic Form, An Introduction*, p.3

After taking in the big picture in terms of choice of form in relation to content zoom in: Explore the stanza form, lineation, punctuation, the use of enjambment and caesura. Single line stanzas draw attention to themselves. If they are end-stopped they can suggest isolation, separation. Couplets imply twoness. Stanzas of three lines are called tercets and feature in villanelles and terzarima. On the page, both these forms tend to look rather delicate, especially if separated from each other by the silence of white space. Often balanced through rhyme, quatrains look a bit more robust and sturdy. Cinquains are swollen quatrains in which the last line often seems to throw the stanza out of balance.

Focus in on specific examples and on points of transition. For instance, if a poem has four regular quatrains followed by a couplet, examine the effect of this change. If we've been ticking along nicely in iambic metre and suddenly trip on a trochee, examine why. Consider regularity. Closed forms of poems, such as sonnets, are highly regular with set rhyme schemes, metre and number of lines. The opposite form is called 'open', the most extreme version of which is free verse. In free verse poems, the poet dispenses with any set metre, rhyme scheme or recognisable traditional form. What stops this sort of poetry from being prose chopped up to look like verse? The care of the design on the page. Hence, we need to focus here on lineation. Enjambment runs over lines and makes connections; caesura pauses a line and separates words. Lots of enjambment generates a sense of the language running away from the speaker. Lots of caesuras generate a halting, hesitant, choppy movement to lines. Opposites, these devices work in tandem and where they fall is always significant in a good poem.

Remember poetic form is never merely decorative. And bear in mind too the fact that the most volatile materials require the strongest containers.

Nice to metre...
A brief guide to metre and rhythm in poetry

Why express yourself in poetry? Why read words dressed up and expressed as a poem? What can you get from poetry that you can't from prose? There are many compelling answers to these questions. Here, though, we're going to concentrate on one aspect of the unique appeal of poetry – the structure of sound in poetry. Whatever our stage of education, we are all already sophisticated at detecting and using structured sound. Try reading the  following sentences without any variation whatsoever in how each sound is emphasised, and they will quickly lose what essential human characteristics they have. The sentences will sound robotic. So, in a sense, we won't be teaching anything new here. It's just that in poetry the structure of sound is carefully unusually crafted and created. It becomes a key part of what a poem is.

We will introduce a few new key technical terms along the way, but the ideas are straightforward. Individual sounds [syllables] are either stressed [emphasised, sounding louder and longer] or unstressed. As well as clustering into words and sentences for meaning, these sounds [syllables] cluster into rhythmic groups or feet, producing the poem's metre, which is the characteristic way its rhythm works.

In some poems, the rhythm is very regular and may even have a name, such as iambic pentameter. At the other extreme a poem may have no discernible regularity at all. As we have said, this is called free verse. It is vital to remember that the sound in a good poem is structured so that it combines effectively with the meanings.

For example, take a look at these two lines from Marvell's *To his Coy Mistress*:

'But at my back I alwaies hear
Times winged Chariot hurrying near:'

Forgetting the rhythms for a moment, Marvell is basically saying at this point 'Life is short, Time flies, and it's after us'. Now concentrate on the rhythm of his words.

- In the first line every other syllable is stressed: 'at', 'back', 'al', 'hear'.
- Each syllable before these is unstressed 'But', 'my', 'I', 'aies'.
- This is a regular beat or rhythm which we could write
  ti TUM / ti TUM / ti TUM / ti TUM , with the / separating the feet. ['Feet' is the technical term for metrical units of sound]
- This type of two beat metrical pattern is called iambic, and because there are four feet in the line, it is tetrameter. So this line is in 'iambic tetrameter'. [Tetra is Greek for four]
- Notice that 'my' and 'I' being unstressed diminishes the speaker, and we are already prepared for what is at his 'back', what he can 'hear' to be bigger than him, since these sounds are stressed.

- On the next line, the iambic rhythm is immediately broken off, since the next line hits us with two consecutive stressed syllables straight off: 'Times' 'wing'. Because a pattern had been established, when it suddenly changes the reader feels it, the words feel crammed together more urgently, the beats of the rhythm are closer, some little parcels of time have gone missing.

A physical rhythmic sensation is created of time slipping away, running out. This subtle sensation is enhanced by the stress-unstress-unstress pattern of words that follow, 'chariot hurrying' [TUM-ti-ti, TUM-ti-ti]. So the hurrying sounds underscore the meaning of the words.

14 ways of looking at a poem

 Though conceived as pre-reading exercises, most of these tasks work just as well for revision.

1. Mash them [1] – mix together lines from two or more poems. The students' task is to untangle the poems from each other.

2. Mash them [2] – the second time round make the task significantly harder. Rather than just mixing whole lines, mash the poems together more thoroughly, words, phrases, images and all, so that unmashing seems impossible. At first sight.

3. Dock the last stanza or few lines from a poem. The students should come up with their own endings for the poem. Compare with the poet's version. Or present the poem without its title. Can the students come up with a suitable one?

4. Break a poem into segments. Split the class into groups. Each group work in isolation on their segment and feedback on what they discover. Then their task is to fit the poem and their ideas about it together as a whole.

5. Give the class the first and last stanza of a poem. Their task is to provide the filling. They can choose to attempt the task at beginner level [in prose] or at world class level [in poetry].

6. Add superfluous words to a poem. Start off with obvious interventions, such as the interjection of blatantly alien, noticeable words. Try smuggling 'pineapple', 'bourbon' and 'haberdashers' into any of the poems and see if you can get it past the critical sensors.

7. Repeat the exercise – This time using much less extravagant words. Try to smuggle in a few intensifiers, such as 'really', 'very' and 'so'. Or extra adjectives.

8. Collapse the lineation in a poem and present it as continuous prose. The students' task is to put it back into verse. Discussing the various pros and cons or various possible arrangements – short lines, long lines, irregular lines - can be very productive. Pay particular attention to line breaks and the words that end them. After a whatever-time-you- deem-fit, give the class the pattern of the first stanza. They then have to decide how to arrange the next stanza. Drip feed the rest of the poem to them.

9. Find a way to present the shapes of each poem on the page without the words. The class should work through each poem, two minutes at a time, speculating on what the shape might tell us about the content of the poem. This exercise works especially well as a starter activity. We recommend you use two poems at a time, as the comparison helps students to recognise and appreciate different shapes.

10. Test the thesis that an astute reader can recognise poems by men from those written by women. Give the class one of the poems, such as *The Laboratory*, *Invictus* or *Genetics* without the name of the poet.

Ask them to identify whether the writer is male or female and to explain their reasons for identifying them as such.

11. Split the class into groups. Each group should focus their analysis on a different feature of the poem. Start with the less obvious aspects: Group 1 should concentrate on enjambment and caesuras; group 2 on punctuation; group 3 on the metre and rhythm; group 4 on function words – conjunctions, articles, prepositions. 2-5 mins. only. Then swap focus, four times. Share findings.

12. In *Observations on Poetry*, Robert Graves wrote that 'rhymes properly used are the good servants whose presence at the dinner-table gives the guests a sense of opulent security; never awkward or over-clever, they hand the dishes silently and professionally. You can trust them not to interrupt the conversation or allow their personal disagreements to come to the notice of the guests; but some of them are getting very old for their work'. Explore the poets' use of rhyme in the light of Graves' comment. Are the rhymes ostentatiously original or old hat? Do they stick out of the poem or are they neatly tucked in? Are they dutiful servants of meaning or noisy disrupters of the peace?

13. The Romantic poet, John Keats, claimed that 'we hate poetry that has a palpable design upon us – and if we do not agree seems to put its hand its breeches pock'. Apply his comment to this selection of poems. Do any seem to have a 'palpable design' on the reader? If so, how does the poet want us to respond?

14. Each student should crunch the poem down to one word per line. Discuss this process as a class. Project the poem so the whole class can see it and start the crunching process by indicating and then crossing-out the function words from each line. Now discuss which of the remaining words is most important. This will also give you an opportunity to refer to grammatical terms, such as nouns and verbs. Once each line has been reduced to one word, from this list, pupils should crunch again. This time all that should remain are the five most important words in the whole poem. Now they need to write two or three sentences for each of these words explaining exactly why they are so important and why the poet didn't choose any of the possible synonyms.

IDENTITY

W. E. Henley [1849-1903], *Invictus*

Late Victorian poet, editor and literary critic, W.E. Henley had to have half a leg amputated while he was still a child, an experience that may have helped to shape his admiration for the sort of stout courage and iron fortitude expressed in his famous poem, *Invictus*, which means 'invincible' in Latin.

Henley's was, of course, the favourite poem of Nelson Mandela who regularly recited it for inspiration during his twenty-seven years of incarceration in Robben Island prison. As the actor Morgan Freeman, who played Mandela in the 2009 film named after the poem, **Invictus**, says, the 'poem was his favourite... When he lost courage, when he felt like just giving up — just lie down and not get up again — he would recite it. And it would give him what he needed to keep going.'

It starts with complete universal darkness, a night that completely 'covers' both the speaker and, in a powerful piece of hyperbole, the whole of the globe, 'from pole to pole'. Ominously, the unrelenting darkness is 'black as the pit', with connotations of hell, an image echoed in the later phrase 'Horror of the shade'. Henley expresses a Late Victorian sceptical mentality; he does not thank the Christian God for his strength, but 'whatever gods may be' [his scepticism signalled by the lower case 'g', the plurals and that hedging verb 'may']. In the final lines he goes, further, declaring in stirringly defiant, undaunted humanist terms that he is the 'captain' of his soul. Clearly the overt meaning is that the poet declares that he, not a priest or higher authority or God, is the custodian of his deepest sense of self. The poet is taking responsibility for himself and his own actions. But the metaphor of 'captain' suggests a soldier or the captain of a vessel of some sorts, both of which imply that the self will continue to be tested in one form of extremis or another and suffer the 'blugeonings of chance'.

The declarative ending of the poem and note of individual defiance expressed in the language is re-enforced by the rhyme scheme, the arrangement of sentences, the stanza form and the metre. The rhymes, for examples are all full, masculine ones, so that each word chimes harmoniously with its partner, creating a sense of sonic resolution and completeness at the end of each stanza. This effect is enhanced by the fact the sentences in each stanza are completed with the stanza's last word, emphasised by a full stop. In addition, the poem's cross-rhyme scheme begins and ends with rhymes for 'soul'. The poem is written in tetrameter, or common metre, which is a metre often used for songs. Four beats match the four line quatrains and the poem also has four stanzas. There is a tension, however, between the regularising shaping form and the metrical irregularity within lines, for, although each line comprises four beats these are sometimes stretched out or condensed and bunched together. Noticeably in the last stanza these metrical irregularities a are ironed out and the lines march confidently forward in regular iambs.

It's the great phrasing that makes *Invictus* such a powerful, memorable poem. The sense of challenges faced down, of suffering, fear, pain and punishment born with courage are made palpable and make the stoical defiance the more admirable. A cloze exercise would help highlight Henley's excellent choices of words to create vivid concrete images.

> Out of the night that covers me,
> Black as the .... from pole to pole,
> I thank whatever gods may be
> For my .... soul.
>
> In the fell .... of circumstance
> I have not winced nor cried aloud.
> Under the .... of chance
> My head is bloody, but ....
>
> Beyond this place of wrath and tears
> Looms but the .... of the shade,
> And yet the menace of the years
> Finds and shall find me ....
>
> It matters not how strait the gate,
> How charged with punishments the scroll,
> I am the master of my fate,
> I am the .... of my soul.

A number of the poems in this anthology explore or express the nature of heroism/ courage/ manliness. *The Charge of the Light Brigade* and *The Man he Killed* spring immediately to mind, both of which, interestingly enough, are Victorian/ early Edwardian poems. From examining these poems what appear to be the most important qualities to a manly Victorian/ Edwardian hero? How might this be different from a modern hero, or a real-life hero, like Nelson Mandela?

As we've said, Henley's poem is a rousing, stirring one. Often teachers put up inspiring quotations around their classrooms. Students could collect these and discuss what makes the quotes effective or not effective. To what extent is the effectiveness dependent on the linguistic qualities of the quote? Students may already have favourite quotations. They could share these or research others.

Invictus crunched:

NIGHT – PIT – GODS – UNCONQUERABLE – CLUTCH – WINCED – BLUDGEONINGS - UNBOWED – BEYOND – HORROR – MENACE – UNAFRAID – NOT – PUNISHMENT – MASTER – SOUL

Robert Frost, *The Road Not Taken*

An ambiguous sigh

Despite this poem being about the 'journey' of life, the verbs associated with the narrator are rather hesitant. Most* are in the past tense and they are static, negative, suggesting fate as well as free will. The narrator's tone is difficult to pin down; the register is informal, the style conversational and voice seems rather matter of fact. The key word is the ambiguous 'sigh' in the final stanza. This could indicate either relief or its opposite, regret. Like the narrator, the reader is presented with two possible roads of interpretation.

The wood and the roads

The wood and the two roads might be considered to be 'setting', but they play so important a role in the poem that it is worth regarding them as characters in the drama. Look at the adjective used to describe the wood. It is a 'yellow' wood and the use of the colour is suggestive. Is yellow being used here in the [American] sense of cowardly? If it is, then is the narrator's journey an attempt to escape? The 'yellow' wood might also be seen as a comment on the season. Is it autumn? If so, the time of year might be relevant to the situation of the narrator; there could be a signal that he will not be able to 'come back.' Whatever the meaning of 'yellow' the colour is  unsettling. It is not fresh and green and the word might be seen as rather sickly.

What associations might we have with woods? The narrator in the poem is alone and being in the woods isolates him. Often configured as the opposite to the home, the wild wood is a place of folklore and myth, an ungoverned space where all sorts of things might happen [think about fairy tales, such as Red Riding Hood or Mirkwood in *The Hobbit*] A wood is also a place where it is hard to see clearly and a place where we can easily get lost. It's in the woods that witches and wolves live and other nasty creatures form stories. Consequently we can see the wood as a place that is not entirely comforting and could even be threatening.

A popular reading of the poem tends to stress the difference between the two roads, but crucially they are 'really about the same'. So, does the time spent making a decision make any difference when there will always be a 'road NOT taken'? Arguably that the appearance of rational decision-making is just a charade. Really his decision was arbitrary; he had no adequate reason to choose one path over another. It was only afterwards that he rationalised it. Unsettlingly, Frost implies that this is how we might make all the decisions in our lives.

The fact that the two roads 'diverge' is striking. The verb implies the increasing impossibility of ever returning, an idea which is developed with the simple phrase 'way leads on to way'. This shows the complexities of life and gives a strong geographical sense of the journey. At the same time, it makes the likelihood of returning ever more remote. 'Diverged' presents the narrator with a stark and absolute choice and the notion of 'the crossroads' has a powerful resonance in American folklore [just look up the life story of the blues guitarist Robert Johnson for a particularly exciting 'crossroads' story!] The line,

'And both that morning equally lay/in leaves no step had trodden black'

seems to indicate that once someone [the narrator] does step down that road, the leaves will be 'trodden black'. The colour imagery suggests that that this spur of the moment decision, made in the yellow wood, may have dark consequences. This is linked with the word 'sigh' in the final stanza which hints at disillusionment... but could, as we've suggested, also be read as a sigh of relief. The unsettling quality of *The Road Not Taken* is shown in the phrase 'where it bent in the undergrowth'. The verb 'bent' gives the road a sinister action and implies straying off the 'straight and narrow.' The fact that the road bends into the 'undergrowth' is also rather unnerving with its hints of concealment.

44

The narrator 'takes the other' which is 'just as fair' [though note, crucially not 'fairer'] despite the negative descriptions of the other path. This could be seen as a use of irony, as the chosen route is similarly threatening. The timeframe is more complicated than it first appears and works best on a time line:

The decision made in the wood	The time the narrator is speaking	The future
↓	↓	↓
Verbs in past tense	I shall be telling this... [anticipates future]	'ages and ages hence'

He has realised that his decision is important and anticipates a future where he will 'sigh'. The poet knows he will be 'telling' his story which seems to place him as a character in his own narrative in a rather cinematic way.

The sound of sense

Robert Frost's verse is accessible and conversational. He wanted to make poems out of ordinary words, following the rhythms of a spoken voice, rather than the rhythms of music. He coined the term 'the sound of sense' to describe these speech rhythms. An American poet, Frost felt that too much contemporary English poetry used tired, out-dated 'poetic' language, such as extravagant or clichéd metaphors. Frost wanted to whittle away tired old poetic style and strip the language clean, and in doing so make his poems accessible to ordinary, non-specialist readers. He also told stories in his poems that are easy to visualise. Despite being precise in terms of setting, his poems also have an appealing universality about them. Though this is Frost's story it relates to every reader who has had to make tricky decisions.

The first thing to notice is that the 'voice' of the narrator is highly distinctive in terms of syntax. Pick out all the examples where the word order is strange or 'quirky'. The narrator also uses conversational links such as 'and', 'though', and 'because'. He interjects with an 'oh', which is informal. There is also careful use of repetition in this poem. This because he knows that 'way leads on to way' and he doubts if he will 'ever come back'. Certain phrases are also repeated 'Two roads diverged.' The first time they diverge

in a 'yellow' wood but by the time he has started to think about the future, it has become just 'a wood'. Its colour is no longer important; what matters is that this is where his decision was made. There is also a repetition of the word '<u>I</u>' in the final stanza. This tiny feature works on a number of levels:

- The 'I' is positioned at the end of line three of the stanza which immediately signals its importance – it forms part of the rhyme scheme.
- BUT it also comes at the very end of the clause 'and I' which seems to hint at his insignificance!
- The 'I' is repeated at the start of the fourth line. This gives a stuttering effect and conveys a sense of uncertainty and ambiguity.
- The sound of the second 'I' also forms an internal rhyme with 'by', consolidating the narrator's place in the narrative.

Song-like form

Scan the first stanza and you will find that there are four stressed beats in each line. Generally speaking the poem is written in iambic tetrameter but there are extra [unstressed] beats which provide a degree of freedom and allow Frost to maintain speech rhythms of a conversational voice.

'Two roads/ diverged/ in a yell/ow wood,

And sor/ry I /could not tra/vel both

And be/ one tra/veller, long/ I stood

And looked/ down one/ as far/ as I could

To where/ it bent/ in the un/dergrowth;'

Here the stresses are emboldened and the feet with the 'extra' unstressed syllables are underlined. This allows Frost the flexibility to write in a naturalistic way. At the same time it enables him to stick mainly to iambic tetrameter, also called common metre, which is the metre of songs and spells.

The poem consists of four stanzas of five lines [quintains] with four beats. Stanzas of five lines are a little unsettling. Four lines suggest balance, regularity and completeness. The extra line works like an unbalancing afterthought. The stanzas seem to come to a neat conclusion, only for there to be another extra, destabilising line. This coming to an apparent conclusion and then undercutting it with doubt embodies in form the main theme of the poem.

The rhyme scheme of the poem is abaab. The cross rhymed lines give a sense of movement and progress, but the enclosure of the rhyming couplets in lines three and four [in an envelope scheme] are a device by which Frost is able to convey a sense of entrapment and inevitability. The rhymes are masculine [the rhymes fall on the stressed beats] with the exception of the feminine final line. This famously enigmatic last line is left unresolved by means of this device. The reader is left uncertain about what 'difference' has been made, and whether crucially Frost, or his narrator, made a good or bad decision.

Enjambment is used to maintain the flow of colloquial speech. It is tempered by the use of caesurae which are like the tiny hesitations a speaker might make as he searches for the right word. So, Frost takes us into the moment of writing the poem and creates a close intimacy between himself and the reader.

Wrong roads?

Frost was forty two when this poem was published in 1916 in the collection Mountain Interval. Although he is seen as an American poet, Frost had by this time taken a huge decision and moved with his family from America to England because of the difficulties he faced finding a publisher in the USA. He had tried his hand at working in a mill, teaching, journalism and farming without a great deal of success and it was the sale of a farm which funded his relocation to England in 1912.

At the time of writing *The Road not Taken*, Frost's English friend, the poet Edward Thomas, was deciding whether to enlist in the British Army which may offer some explanation about the subject matter of the poem. Although it seems fair to say that Frost had already had considerable experience of making life changing decisions.

Frost said of this poem that 'you have to be careful of that one; it's a tricky poem...very tricky.' Some readers have assumed the choice of the road was the right one, others that it was the wrong one. To do either surely misses the point; the poem hovers between the two readings, and resists being reduced to one perspective. That's the point.

The Road Not Travelled crunched:

YELLOW – SORRY – TRAVELLER – FAR – UNDERGROWTH – FAIR – CLAIM – GRASSY – PASSING – SAME – MORNING – BLACK – DRY – KNOWING – DOUBTED – SIGH – AGES – DIVERGED – LESS – DIFFERENCE

D.H. Lawrence, Piano

Appassionato

Although he was an accomplished and influential poet, D.H. Lawrence [1885-1930] is probably most famous for his controversial novels, such as *Sons and Lovers*, *Women in Love* and, in particular, *Lady Chatterley's Lover*. Born into a working-class mining family in Nottinghamshire in the late Victorian period, Lawrence was a prodigious and distinctly original artist who also wrote essays, short stories and plays. He remains a highly controversial figure because in addition to expressing radically right wing political views, in his novels Lawrence explored sexuality in a frank manner that was deeply shocking to his contemporaries. Famously when *Lady Chatterley's Lover* was finally published in England in 1960, thirty years after Lawrence's death, its publishers, Penguin, were prosecuted under the Obscene Publications Act. Notoriously Lawrence's novel depicts a passionate sexual relationship between an upper-class lady and her working-class gardener. Despite the controversy, the literary qualities of the novel led to an acquittal that changed the nature of what could be published in England.

Give me five

Recently the poet and academic Simon Armitage has recommended a strategy for reading a poem that avoids the pitfalls of technique spotting. Armitage suggests that readers pick out around five words or so from a poem and then explore meticulously why the poet may have chosen these specific words rather than synonyms that may have served nearly as well. So, let's try applying the Armitage method to Lawrence's *Piano*, but with a slight variation. As well as individual words, we're going to choose a phrase or two. Which five words or phrases jump out from the rest of the poem and demand our attention? Pick these for yourself before reading any

further. And don't be tempted into peaking at our selection before you've made your own. That'd be cheating. Go on, get the poem right now and pick out your best five words. Don't you dare read ahead until you've done this. We're watching you...

For us, the following words stand out: 'boom'; 'insidious mastery', 'betrays', 'glamour', 'manhood' and 'weep'. We know, we know, that's six. We cheated, just a little. The explosive, onomatopoeic first word in the list, 'boom' seems out of place in a poem describing a woman singing accompanied by a pianist. In the first word of the first quatrain Lawrence had established that the music is playing 'softly' and immediately after 'boom' refers to 'tingling strings'. With its internal rhyme and 'i' sound, sonically that phrase is much lighter than the deeper 'boom'. So, is this just a not very good description perhaps? Maybe, but perhaps 'boom' conveys something of the profound effect of the experience on the poet - it sets off an explosion in his head. Moreover, the sonic tension here echoes a wider tension in the poem in terms of the ambivalent way in which Lawrence presents this experience and, indeed, himself as a character.

Insidious mastery

The second phrase we've selected, for instance, suggests that the experience had a powerful effect, 'mastery', but also an unwelcome one. Normally something 'insidious' has a harmful effect. Moreover, carried over from its Middle French origins the adjective suggests deceit, cunning, treachery and even entrapment. If the memory of a piano playing were a pleasant one, taking Lawrence back to fond childhood memories, why does he use such a negatively charged word? Initially the poet could maintain some emotional distance from the memory the music prompts. He says that he 'sees' 'a child' sitting under the piano. While this is clearly himself, Lawrence remains an observer; he could, for instance, have written 'I am a child again sitting under the piano'. However, by the second stanza this distance between the observer and the observed, the adult poet and his childhood self, has collapsed. The third person 'a child' has transformed into 'me', and furthermore into the 'very heart of me'.

Why does Lawrence resist the tug of the music and the memories it triggers? Why is the effect 'insidious'? It is 'in spite' of himself that the song 'betrays him'. Like 'insidious', 'betray' seems an incongruous and disproportionate word in this context, and like 'insidious' it implies treachery, back-stabbing, harm done. So, it seems Lawrence feels mastered and overwhelmed by the power of song which unlocks memories and releases a surge of strong emotions. Neither his reason nor his will are strong enough to hold back the tide or 'flood' of feelings. And these feelings are so potent because they are of loss and displacement, specifically the loss of a secure, familiar home, the loss of a stable centre of being. This is why the experience is 'insidious' and feels like a betrayal.

Winter inside

Home offered protection; a metaphorical 'winter' was kept 'outside'. It provided comfort too - it was 'cosy'. Moreover, it set a clear sense of direction, purpose and perhaps morality - the 'tinkling piano' was his 'guide'. Notice too the plural pronoun in contrast to the lonely 'I' of earlier in the poem. In photography, a negative is the black and white image from which colour prints used to be  produced. Bright objects in real life appear dark on a negative and vice versa. Reverse the positive details of the home and we get the negative image of what Lawrence wants, but longer has in his life. So, we understand that now, as an adult, the poet feels rootless, unsupported, exposed to the coldness and harshness of a metaphorical winter, desperate, lost and alone. And to add to his woe, he is aware that the bright, warm image of home is in the past, it has gone from him forever and cannot be recovered. And these negatives feelings sweep over him via the music. No wonder then that he resisted their effect.

It might seem odd that Lawrence describes childhood as having a 'glamour'. Possibly rather than the modern associations with celebrity lifestyles, by 'glamour' he means brightness and attractiveness. Perhaps too Lawrence is drawing on older meanings of the word of 'enchantment' and 'magic' which fit with the sense that he has become entranced by the music, memory and emotion. If 'glamour' signals a positive dimension to the experience, his negative feelings are evident in the fact that he describes his susceptibility as emasculating and infantilising. He felt 'mastered' and his 'manhood' is, he says, 'cast down' when he caves into, feels defeated by raw emotion. Clearly, then the poet's feelings are ambivalent.

What impression do you form of Lawrence's character from this poem? He wants to convey a tough manliness that can resist the annoyingly noisy 'clamour' for his attention of the 'great black piano', despite it being played 'appassionato'. Despite his strength, he is, however, mastered.

Such is the power of music, of memory and of emotion. Hence while protesting that he has been betrayed by his feelings the poet simultaneously demonstrates a sensitive, emotional artistic self. Tough and sensitive at the same time. Perhaps this self-conscious self-projection helps explain the inconsistent identification of the poem's speaker with his childhood self. A little distance creeps back into the perspective in the concluding image, for example: 'I weep like a child for the past'. It may also help to explain the mastery Lawrence establishes over the material. While the poem has a lot of enjambment, which suggests the language is flowing free from constraint, like the flood of emotion, this is boxed in and contained by neat, orderly quatrains. And these orderly quatrains each end reassuring with emphatic full stops. If there is a flood, the flood defences appear able to cope. So, for a poem about emotion flooding and overwhelming the manly defences of reason and will, it's a remarkably composed, controlled affair. Tough, manly but also sensitive too.

Piano crunched:

SINGING – SEE – CHILD – MOTHER – INSIDIOUS – BETRAYS – HOME – GUIDE – VAIN – GLAMOUR – MANHOOD - WEEP

Louis MacNeice, Prayer before Birth

What's the most unusual narrative perspective you've come across in a novel, short story or poem? Recently the novelist Ian McEwan has re-written the story of *Hamlet* from the perspective of the prince as a foetus in his betraying mother's womb. Clearly this choice of point of view is more of a challenge on the large scale or a novel than it is on the miniature one of a poem. But why choose this perspective, or any unusual or alien perspective in the first place? The point, surely, is to show us something familiar in a new light, from a new angle. According to the influential Russian Formalist critic, the marvellously named, Vicktor Schlovsky the repetitive nature of modern life and modern habits deaden our responsiveness to the world around us. Literature 'defamiliarises' the world to refresh our appreciation and understanding of it. Okay, but why write specifically from the perspective of a foetus?

Well, clearly, we associate babies with innocence and purity. As yet, the poem's narrator has not been touched, or perhaps contaminated, by interaction with the outside world. And because they're pre-birth they express fear and concern about the impact the world might have on that innocence. A foetus is also entirely vulnerable, incapable of defending itself, reliant entirely on the protective instincts it elicits in others. Though, we are all always developing, the younger we are the faster the rate of development, so foetus's are especially impressionable and malleable, their development shaped by their environment in a more profound way than older people are. In MacNeice's poem the foetus will become what the world turns it into.

The black racks

And the world appears a frightening, threatening place in this poem. The opening stanza introduces fear of nasty beasts, both natural and supernatural. These are the fears of a child's imagination, 'blood-sucking bats' and 'club-footed ghouls'. These monsters soon give way to a more

disturbing source of fear, humans. Rather than nurture or care or love or protect the new-born baby, the narrator fears the world will imprison, drug, trick and torture it on 'black racks' and 'roll' it in 'blood-baths'. The fears escalate alarmingly as the imagery becomes gruesome. The third stanza provides some respite, with images of a better, kinder, more nurturing world, one that is rooted in nature. But this respite doesn't last long. Soon MacNeice is describing how we have to play different 'parts' like actors in our own lives, how we have to endure lectures and hectoring, put up with being laughed and frowned and cursed at, even by our own children. He also warns of the dangers of men who are bestial or fanatical. And in the fourth stanza the speaker expresses a deep sense of helplessness.

The change of verb in the opening refrain to, 'I am not yet born; forgive me' signals that the violence, damage and sin are inevitable and inescapable. Throughout the fourth stanza the individual's lack of agency is emphasised. The child will become like a puppet, driven and controlled by external forces: 'The sins in me the world shall commit'; 'when they murder by means of my hands'. A similar idea is expressed in seventh stanza where the poem's speaker imagines themselves transformed into a killing machine, a 'lethal automaton'. Lacking individuality, stripped of free-will and self-determination, dehumanised as a 'thing' and diminished to just a 'cog' in a 'machine', the speaker becomes a weapon primed for someone else's use. The fact that the  forces dragooning, using and controlling the speaker are a faceless, anonymous 'they' and 'those' makes them more sinister. We are not given any sense of who or what these forces are; we only know the individual cannot resist their power and that their power will be abusive.

The poem ends with three similes expressing the speaker's fear that they will become helplessly insignificant: They will be blown around like 'thistledown', so lacking in humanity they will be like a 'stone' and so insubstantial that they could be spilt like 'water'. The unformed malleability of the speaker is underlined by the fact that he/she transforms from a machine, to a cog, to down, to water and to a stone in the space of a few lines. Bleakly, rather than accept this fate, the speaker moves into imperative mode, addressing the reader directly with the short, blunt phrase, 'Otherwise kill me'. After this truncated final line there is nothing but white space.

Engine of hope

The content of the poem might be rather bleak, but it's delivered with an energy that hints at the capacity of the individual to resist and shape their own destiny. To see how the rhythmical aspect of the poem works, we'll take one example, and look at it in some detail. Here's the second stanza with the stressed syllables in bold:

'I **fear** that the **hum**an **race** may with **tall walls wall** me,
with **strong drugs dope** me, with **wise lies lure** me,
on **black racks rack** me, in **blood-baths roll** me'

The metre here is irregular, shifting between the first line and the following two. It starts with a skipping rhythm, generated by a combination of an anapaestic pattern [unstress, unstress, stress] with clearly unstressed words ['that the' and 'may with'] which make the rhythm more pronounced. The end of this line, and the following ones, are more stressy, as five times in a row stressed words are piled up consecutively. The effect is enhanced by MacNeice's use of internal rhymes such as 'tall walls' and 'black racks' and alliteration, such as 'drugs dope' and 'lies lure'. Forming a rapid and repeated DUM-DUM-DUM-dum pattern, these individual stressed monosyllables sound like bullets in a volley of gunfire - 'tall walls wall me'; 'strong drugs dope me'; 'black racks rack me'.

Great energy and rhetorical momentum is generated by the combination of metre, syntax and word choices. And the metrical pattern that runs throughout the poem, albeit with some variations, is MacNeice's invention, an expression of creative freedom and individuality. This muscular counterforce is also embodied in the poem's stanza form. Noticeably the stanzas grow in length, like a new baby and their form is irregular. Two stanzas are tercets and two are quatrains, with others ranging from a couplet to ten lines. And even their growth is irregular, in fits and starts, with the sixth stanza, for example, bucking the general pattern of increasing length. Similarly, though the stanzas grow longer, towards the end the lines actually shorten. Apart from in the first line of each stanza the lineation also follows no pre-set order or regularised pattern. Hence the poem's development is not predictable.

O hear me

It as if the narrator of the poem, the unborn foetus, is pleading with us to intervene and help or even save them from the degradations of the world. The verbs, 'hear', 'console', 'provide' and so forth suggest a parental responsibility in the reader. Neediness may be toughened up by the imperative form, but there is a sense of desperation. This is particularly evident when MacNeice uses apostrophes, such as the repeated 'O hear me'. That naked, single syllable implies pain and need. 'Hear' is repeated as this suggests that normally we don't listen to the weakest, the most vulnerable and the most innocent. Mostly the speaker seeks protection. But in the third stanza a more positive vision is briefly imagined. The innocent, unborn child's needs are presented as simple, natural sustaining things, such as 'water' and 'grass'. Nature also provides company and the child is so in tune with the natural world that the sky 'sings' to it. This is a rural idyll, a natural sanctuary

60

in stark contrast to the oppressive stanzas that surround it. As in Romantic poetry, Nature also is a moral compass, 'a white light' that is internalised as a 'guide' through the world of experience.

References to innocence and experience and to Romantic poetry might bring William Blake, author of *The Tyger*, to mind. Rejecting the doctrine of original sin, Blake and other Romantics, believed children were innocents, closer to God than adults. Often in Blake's poetry, in particular, interaction with society corrupts the innocent. Though in this way MacNeice's poem could be seen to continuing a long established poetic theme, it also directly reflects the world and the period in history in which the poet wrote it. In the middle of the

twentieth century the world was divided by violently opposed political ideologies. The Second World War was a war between countries, but it was also a war of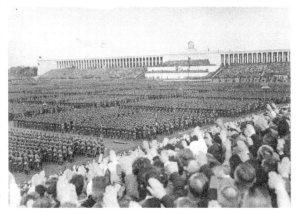
political ideologies, Fascism vs. communism and liberal democracy. When whole nations and their governments adopt extreme political ideologies that are as potent as any fanatical religion and only the strongest of individuals are able to resist the pull of the group. Others become 'lethal automatons', suppressing their natural human empathy, carrying out orders unthinkingly, like prison guards at concentration camps. The fact that this foetusis aware of the dangers gives it a chance of avoiding these patterns, and instead finding and expressing its own individual self.

Prayer Before Birth crunched:

HEAR - BLOODSUCKING - GHOUL - CONSOLE - WALL - DOPE -
LIES - RACK - YET - WATER - BIRDS - GUIDE - FORGIVE - SINS -
THEY - TREASON - MURDER - MY - REHEARSE - PARTS -
LECTURE - LAUGH - FOLY - DOOM - CURSE - O - GOD - NEAR -
FILL - STRENGTH - AUTOMATON - COG - THING - DISSIPATE -
THISTLEDOWN - THITHER - WATER - SPILL - STONE - KILL

Written during the Second World War, MacNeice's poem presents a pretty

 bleak picture of the world the foetus will enter and of the various malign effects it will have. How about writing your own version of the poem? Either you could update it to the world of President Trump, North Korea and crises in our public services, or you could put a more positive spin on what the world has in store for someone born into it today.

Gillian Clarke, *Catrin*

Love me tender

If we were to imagine a poem about the relationship between a mother and her daughter we might expect something rather tender, perhaps even soppy or sentimental. If the poem was written from the point of view of the mother and was addressed to the daughter whose name formed the title that would add further weight to these expectations. And if the poem explored the mother daughter relationship through the memory of the child as a new-born baby, we'd be fairly convinced we were going to get something sweet and affectionate. After all, the daughter could and probably would read the poem. Boldly Clarke's seemingly autobiographical poem confounds such expectations. Rather than the sorts of motherly words we might expect - care, love, gentle, hope etc. Clarke's poem is full of words from the semantic field of warfare, such as 'confrontation', 'fought', 'struggle', 'shouted', 'fighting', 'defiant', 'conflict'. Indeed, the first memory of her daughter, her birth is described as 'our first / fierce confrontation'.

Love me true

The central metaphor in Clarke's conversational poem is of the umbilical cord described as a 'tight/ red rope of love' over which 'both' mother and daughter 'fought'. The sonic qualities of this description reinforce the sense: assonance links 'rope', 'both' and 'over'; alliteration connects 'red and rope' and there is a condensed, packed quality to the run of stressed short monosyllables arranged so close together - 'the tight/ red rope of love' [stressed syllables in bold]. The rope metaphor crops up in both stanzas, the first time during the description of childbirth and then later once the daughter has grown into a teenager. This suggests that though the literal, physical link has been cut between mother and child and a deeper, metaphorical level they are still inextricably tied to each other. Describing the umbilical cord as a rope and an 'old' one or a 'red' one is especially unromantic and dehumanising; it may signal the enduring strength of the connection, for rope is thicker than a cord, but not necessarily in a good sense. In both instances, Clarke refers to 'tightness' suggesting proximity, discomfort and perhaps even entrapment. Rope 'tightening' about the speaker's 'life' makes us think not just of constriction, but strangulation. If this all sounds rather alarming, the end of the first stanza does little to alleviate our fears for this relationship.

Clarke tells us that she 'coloured the clean squares' of the hospital room with the 'wild, tender circles' of their 'struggle to become separate'. Perhaps the colouring is a polite way to suggest swearing, as in colourful language. The fact that her words were written 'all over the walls' implies her desperation and the pain of childbirth. 'Circles' implies going round and round without getting anywhere and thus with the rope image signals a form of entrapment. The tussle between mother and daughter is embodied in the language Clarke uses. Like the mother and child, the language at the end of the first stanza pulls in two different directions at the same time and cannot break free of its own contradictions. It is, for example, 'our struggle', a shared, common experience, but they are trying to become 'separate'. The following pronouns further fuse the mutual connection despite the words expressing the desire to be different: 'We want, we shouted' to be 'ourselves'.

We will never part

If we were in any doubt, the second stanza opens with a line that makes the existential conflict between mother and child explicit: 'Neither won nor lost the struggle'. And 'still', apparently many years later, the mother must defend herself from the daughter as if she is under intense physical attack, 'still I am fighting/ you off'. The expression on the daughter's face, her 'defiant glare' suggests  both animosity and a continuing struggle over authority. And this defiance is over a small issue, being allowed to 'skate' for just an hour longer. This might make us worry about what would happen if something more important was at stake. The situation seems potentially explosive.

However, hostility doesn't fill the whole picture. Perhaps we can read some of the words and images differently. Tightness, for instance, can be a positive thing, indicating emotional closeness and intimacy. Noticeably the poem doesn't feature any other characters, only the anonymous people waiting at the traffic lights. There's no father/ husband figure, no male presence or doctors or extended family or siblings. Just the two principle characters, as if they are each other's entire worlds. The speaker's cries were described as 'wild' but the adjective is tempered and modified by the more motherly 'tender'. As the plural personal pronouns ['our', 'we'] signalled, mother and daughter are also alike; the both 'want' their independent sense of identity, both 'shouted'. They're also a match for each other and fight to a stalemate. Isn't there a touch of admiration too in the description of the teenage daughter? A bit of pride in those four adjectives describing her 'straight, strong, long/ brown' hair. Moreover like 'wild' the 'defiant glare' is softened by the warmer adjective 'rosy'. The daughter might be defiant, but she is still polite enough to 'ask' rather than demand that she be allowed to stay out later. Finally, that 'old rope' metaphor is dragged up from another metaphorical place, 'the heart's pool'. The connection between mother and daughter lies in the watery seat of love, or, perhaps, the reservoir of the heart. And the clincher is that it trails not just 'conflict' but 'love'.

Just the two of us

What about the form of Clarke's poem - two free verse stanzas, rather top heavy? What might this suggest? Perhaps the relationship between mother and child, one still slightly bigger and more dominant than the other. Or maybe the stanza structure reflects the dominance of the formative experience of childhood in shaping this tender, competitive, loving, struggling, mutual, dependent, strained, but also loving relationship between a strong mother and daughter just as strong.

Catrin crunched:

REMEMBER - WHITE - WATCHING - PEOPLE - TURN - FIRST - CONFRONTATION - ROPE - FOUGHT - DISINFECTED - WROTE - OVER - COLOURED - TENDER - STRUGGLE - WE - OURSELVES - NEITHER - FEELINGS - CHANGED - OFF - STRONG - ROSY - DEFIANT - HEART'S - TIGHTENING - LOVE - ASK - MORE

How would you feel if you were the daughter in this poem? The poem is set up so that we're placed in her perspective - 'I can remember you', the poet tells us. Perhaps you could research how Clarke's daughter reacted, or better still, imagine her reaction. Either you could write a letter expressing your thoughts and feelings about the poem and about your mother writing about your relationship in this frank, unsentimental way in a poem published and read by other people. Or, if you're really ambitious you could compose a response in verse...

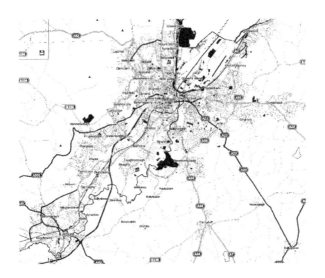

Ciaran Carson, *Belfast Confetti*

Psychogeography

noun

- the study of the influence of geographical environment on the mind or on behaviour.

- the geographical environment of a particular location, typically a city, considered with regard to its influence on the mind or on behaviour.

The city of Belfast is a central topic in the poetry of Belfast-born Northern Irish poet, academic and musician, Ciaran Carson. Not so much Belfast as it is today, two decades after the Northern Irish Peace Process led to ceasefire between Catholic and Protestant paramilitaries and the withdrawal of British troops from Northern Ireland, more the city before and during the period of violence and civil strife known as 'The Troubles'. We haven't the time or the space here to offer a potted history of 'The Troubles' and you can and should

68

research this context yourself as it's vital to a proper understanding of Carson's poem. Suffice it to say that at the time Carson wrote *Belfast Confetti* [1990] the city was deeply divided along sectarian lines, with distinctly Catholic areas, distinctly Protestant areas and a few mixed areas. Such was the hostility between the two communities that it could be dangerous to stray into enemy territory, for a Catholic to find him or herself in a Protestant area and vice versa. Paramilitary groups, such as the Catholic IRA and the Protestant UDF and UVF, continued a cycle of violence attacks and reprisals. The British Army and the local police enforced the rule of law and Northern Ireland was governed from Westminster by a Conservative government.

Carson is one of a group of great writers who emerged at around the same time as each other in Ireland. A slightly older generation of poets included the Nobel Prize-winner, Seamus Heaney and among Carson's contemporaries are Paul Muldoon and Eavan Boland. One way or another, these Irish poets felt compelled to write about 'The Troubles'. But it was a dangerous topic, literally dangerous, as paramilitaries and their supporters could take violent exception to any work of literature that expressed the 'wrong' views. The words you used, your name, the place names you referred to, the images you drew on, all these aspects could be read in terms of political and sectarian allegiances. Even Ciaran Carson's own name, for instance, might arouse suspicion and hostility from both sides of the divide combining as it does a protestant surname with a catholic first name.

The rumble and the rumpus

So, how does Carson present himself as a character within the Northern Irish conflict? In *Belfast Confetti* he appears as a bemused, disorientated and frightened witness. The first word of the poem, the adverb 'suddenly' conveys the out-of-the-blue unexpectedness of violence breaking out. What exactly is happening? It's difficult to tell; the poem, like the situation it  describes is confusing. A riot squad is moving in, so we know a riot is probably breaking out. It appears improvised weapons are being thrown at the riot squad, as it is 'raining' 'nuts, bolts, nails, car-keys'. However, this detritus might have been projected from 'an explosion'. In the melee, it's impossible to tell. There's a 'burst of rapid' machine gun fire. Adding to the confusion, for the reader, is Carson's metamorphising of these objects into aspects of language, 'exclamation marks', 'broken type', 'an asterisk', 'this hyphenated line'. Try removing this extended metaphor, or conceit, from the first four lines: Though the scene remains presented in a confusing, fragmentary, snap-shot style, it's far easier to establish what's happening. So why does Carson use the conceit? What does it add or achieve? Firstly, the punctuation imagery creates a surreal effect. There is something dream-like about imagining exclamation marks raining from the sky. It reminds me of a painting by the surrealist artist René Magritte where bowler-hatted men fall from the sky as rain. The imagery defamiliarises the scene - this means it is presented in an unusual way in order that we can see it in new ways. Thirdly, the imagery conflates writing with the physical world, confusing the conventional and expected relationship between the two. Usually writing attempts to capture or express reality; here it seems reality is composed of bits of text. And it's fragmentary, incomplete, only the functional bits of text - we have a deluge of exclamation marks, 'broken' type, a 'hyphenated line', but, crucially, no words. This takes us back to our narrator, the poet. His arrival in the poem is delayed until the fourth line, as if he is a minor detail in the situation. The imagery in the poem signals the difficulty he is having in finding language up to the task of capturing the complex, dangerous and confusing situation he finds himself in: It makes him think of bits of punctuation, but not of words. He tells us as much in the fifth line where he struggles to 'complete a sentence' but is unable to because it keeps 'stuttering'. Indeed, even by the end of the poem, the poet seems to have failed to form the sentence that might have put this experience into some kind of order.

We haven't mentioned the poem's title. It's another aspect of the poem that initially is difficult for readers to decipher. We might expect something celebratory to follow from a poem with 'confetti' in its title – a wedding, presumably. But, in fact, this is an ironic Northern Irish, or perhaps, Belfast term, for the shrapnel thrown at the riot squad. The title summaries the violence of Belfast during 'The Troubles' and also reveals a kind of grim, ironic humour. Simultaneously it also highlights the issue of coded language, language that has specific meanings only for those inside the culture.

Lost in his own compositional thoughts while a bomb goes off in the background, the poet seems a rather detached and distracted figure. But he is crucial, because we're seeing the situation through his perceptions. The final line of the first stanza cements the conflation of perception, language and physical reality:

'All the alleyways and side streets blocked with stops and colons'

The line conveys the narrator's sense of entrapment in a dangerous and violent space. At the same time, it suggests the routes of his own thoughts are also trapped and blocked, and hence so too is his capacity to describe reality.

Now, in fact, that line we quoted above isn't presented on the page like that. Like every other long, stretched line in the poem, it is broken so that the word 'colon' appears separately. Why do you think Carson set the poem out like this? If you're teaching the poem, you could present it first as continuous prose and get the pupils to re-arrange it the way they think would be most effective. They can then compare and contrast their arrangements with Carson's. We'll return to this structural feature later in this essay.

A fusillade of questions

The second stanza follows a similar pattern to the first, but there is more clarity and clarification. This time the presence of the poet is foregrounded and we start with a reassuring degree of certainty: 'I know this labyrinth so well'. This place is familiar to the narrator who can reel off the names of its streets. On the other hand, the reference to a labyrinth might be alarming - in classical literature it was the place where the Minotaur devoured its victims. The fear of entrapment is made explicit, 'why can't I escape?' and the stanza becomes increasingly hurried and panicky. For example, the truncated sentence, 'dead end again' implies that the speaker is trying to find a way out. He stumbles on armed police. Readers unfamiliar with the technical terms might take a while to process the significance of the list of 'A Saracen. Kremlin-2 mesh. Makrolon face-shields'. But we don't need to know precisely what these are to realise they are ominous and frightening things to find anywhere, but mostly especially on the familiar streets of your home town. Noticeably, Carson lists things, not people - high-tech. defensive or offensive equipment, not policemen - and this makes the scene more inhuman and even more frightening. This list is separated by full stops, suggesting the speed with which the narrator takes in these details, like snap-shots, and it reinforces the overall patterns of fragmentation and defamiliarisation that dominate the whole poem.

Once we know that a Saracen was an armoured vehicle like the one pictured here, we understand more clearly how terrifying the experience must have been. Certainly, we've come a long way and quickly from the opening description of exclamatory rain. Things continue to move swiftly as the soldiers

or police fire a 'fusillade' of urgent stop-and-search type questions. The poet must explain who he is, where he comes from, where he was going. As the weapon imagery makes clear, Carson is still in danger, in danger of being viewed as a potential enemy. And the poem leaves this terrifying situation unresolved. We do not hear of how the poet escaped from a violent scene that had rapidly escalated into something nightmarish.

So, Carson presents himself as a confused, frightened and helpless bystander, trapped in a familiar place that has suddenly become horribly unfamiliar. The experience is so troubling it prompts a crisis in the poet. Those stop-and-search questions, for instance, could have been punctuated to indicate they were spoken by the police/army. Without speech marks they seem to emanate from the poet himself, as if his own identity and purpose has been thrown into almost existential uncertainty. His lack of control is emphasised too through the sense that the scene is being written by some other mysterious force other than the poet who fails to complete his own sentence. A poet's skill is in shaping language; but in this scene even punctuation marks seem actively hostile to the poet. And a line like 'every move is punctuated' prompts the question 'punctuated' by what or whom?

The city as a palimpsest

At the start of this essay I implied that Carson could be conceived of as a sort of poetic psychogeographer, mapping out the psychological experience of living in Belfast. Carson is not just interested in exploring how the city appears in the contemporary world, however, he also delves into how Belfast's shapes and forms, its buildings and streets, its stories and language, continue to be moulded by its history. So, he's a kind of psycho-historian too. The place names, in this poem, for example, are highly significant. All the streets named are off the Catholic Falls Road, which means the riot is taking place in a Catholic area. This is a territory Carson knows 'so well' because he grew up on Raglan street. This area was, and is, his home.

Look up the names of these streets and you'll discover they are all connected with the Crimean War [1853-56]: Balaclava and Inkerman were battles, Crimea and Odessa are places where the war took place and Lord Raglan was an English cavalry officer, famous or infamous, for his pivotal role in the destruction of the Light Brigade, as dramatised in Tennyson's poem. So British colonial history and British military triumphs [and disasters] are written into the fabric of an area of Belfast that is Catholic. This is a form of deep cultural occupation and a potent legacy of British imperialism. Through these associations with a historical conflict the street names also highlight the enduring, repeating pattern of conflict in relations between countries and cultures.

A palimpsest is a piece of writing on which new writing has been superimposed, sometimes erasing the original script. Carson's Belfast is like a palimpsest; the map of the city is constantly re-written and written over time and time again, not least by the poet himself. This map doesn't just represent reality; it constructs the city and shapes our perceptions of it.

In the eyes of Northern Irish paramilitaries and their supporters there was no such thing as an innocent bystander. Through the twin barrels of sectarianism, Carson's presentation of himself as helpless, confused and uncertain would look like weakness, an excuse for not taking one side or another in the conflict. Why, for instance, doesn't he either join the  riot, or side with the police? In the context of iron-clad political views and cast-iron allegiances, it must have taken great courage for Carson, like other Irish poets, artists and musicians, to stand apart and to present themselves as non-partisans.

Belfast Confetti crunched:

RIOT-SQUAD - EXPLOSION - MAP - SENTENCE - BLOCKED - LABYRINTH - ESCAPE - SARACEN - QUESTION-MARKS

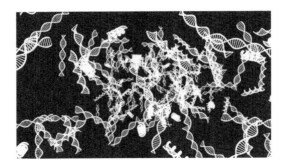

Sinéad Morrissey, *Genetics*

A dancing form

Describe the poetic form of a villanelle in words and it sounds fiendishly difficult to write. Here are the authors of *The Making of a Poem, a Norton Anthology of Poetic Forms* giving it their best shot:

'Five stanzas occur of three lines each. They are followed by a stanza, a quatrain, of four lines. This is common to all villanelles. The first line of the first stanza serves as the last line of the second and fourth stanzas. The third line of the first stanza serves as the last line of the third and fifth stanzas. And these two refrain lines reappear to constitute the last two lines of the closing quatrain...The rhyme scheme is aba, for the first three lines of the poem. And these rhymes reappear to match and catch the refrains, throughout the villanelle. The first line of the first stanza rhymes with the third line of the fourth stanza. And so on.'[2]

 Got it? Good. So your task now is to write your own villanelle. Except that even the complex form of the villanelle seems to

[2] Strand & Boland, *The Making of a Poem*, p. 7

have bewitched even the august authors of the Norton guide. Because that's not quite right. The rhyme scheme in a villanelle is, indeed, aba, but this scheme runs through all the five three line, tercet, stanzas before finally being recycled in the concluding two lines. In other words, all the rhymes in a villanelle are composed from just two rhyme sounds. Lines, 1, 3, 4, 6, 7, 9, 10, 12, 13, 15, 16, 18 & 19 all rhyme with each other. The middle lines of each tercet, lines 2, 5, 8, 11, 14 and 17, also all rhyme with each other. Clearer now? Good. So your task in to write your own villanelle. Except that, we think it's much easier to appreciate the form of a villanelle through a visual representation, thus:

Line 1	A	1st refrain
Line 2	B	
Line 3	A	2nd refrain
Line 4	A	
Line 5	B	
Line 6	A	1st refrain [same as line 1]
Line 7	A	
Line 8	B	
Line 9	A	2nd refrain [same as line 3]
Line 10	A	
Line 11	B	
Line 12	A	1st refrain [same as lines 1 & 6]
Line 13	A	
Line 14	B	
Line 15	A	2nd refrain [same as lines 3 & 9]

Line 16	A	
Line 17	B	
Line 18	A	1st refrain [same as lines 1,6 & 12]
Line 19	A	2nd refrain [same as lines 3, 9 & 15]

Righto. Now you've seen the form, time for you...except that, it helps to try to think of a suitable subject that might fit this elegant, looping dance of a form with its repeated patterns of lines. What we need is a subject in which there is a lot of repetition, but with variations. How about a school day? And though the form looks devilishly difficult, actually once you've got your first three lines you've already written nearly half your poem, including the last two lines. I find it helpful to write these lines in once you've got your first three in place.

And this is how I'd teach Morrissey's poem. Give the students the title and the first stanza only:

'My father's in my fingers, but my mother's in my palms.
I lift them up and look at them with pleasure –
I know my parents made me by my hands.'

So, now we can also slot lines 6, 9,1 2, 15, 18 & 19 into their fixed place in the scheme. We have our two rhyme sounds, 'a' and 'er'. Noticeably Morrissey has already bent the sound a little, or subverted the form a touch, with the assonantal rhyme 'hands' not quite harmonising with the first long 'a' sound. Why might she have done this? Certainly the slight dissonance suits the topic; the poet is trying to bring together parents who have grown apart.

There's a suggestion of slight tension in the poem's sound world. Brought together in their daughter, the parents are also modified in her. So, the poem's rhymes encode the sense of continuity, but also change.

Before going on to fill in the blank lines of the poem, it's worth stopping and discussing the first tercet in more detail. Though the language looks straightforward enough, a gently surreal quality is generated by semantic ambiguity. For example, initially the apostrophes seem to indicate possession and so two nouns appear to be missing. My father's something - 'pen' perhaps? The mildly disorientating effect is sustained in the second line with ambiguous referencing of the twice used pronoun 'them'. Do the two 'thems' refer to the same thing/ person? A number of different possible meaning are kept in play. <u>Which of the following do you think is most convincing?</u>

- I lift the things belonging to my father and mother and look at these
- I lift my hands and look at my hands
- I lift my parents and look at my parents
- I lift my hands and look at my parents

It's only in the last line that the ambiguity is resolved. We realise that the apostrophes are not working to indicate possession but instead to abbreviate the nouns, so that the sense is 'my father is in my fingers'. But there's still a curious, surreal feel here; how can your father be 'in' your fingers or your mother 'in' your palms?

Now you might well be thinking I'm making quite a meal of this. And you could well be right. But I do think it's striking that although Morrissey uses very straightforward diction she manages to make language elusive, hard to pin down in terms of meanings. The double use of 'them' implies that there is no difference between her hands and her parents, they are both simply 'them'. And the overt sentiment of the poem is that her parents can be reunited in her hands. This semantic slipperiness, like the half-rhyme, conveys a counter current or undercurrent in the poem that suggests reconciliation may not be so easy, or perhaps signals the poet's awareness that the reconciliation she achieves is not completely convincing.

It's worth noting too how Morrissey flexes the villanelle form a little. With only two rhyme sounds to play with, rhymes can rather stick out awkwardly from a villanelle, making the language sound unnatural, clunky and too contrived. In an unsubtly written villanelle we will hit and notice the rhymes too much. Morrissey uses enjambment to bed down and tuck in her rhymes, so that the sentence runs over the end of the line and into the next one. In fact the first enjambment runs stanza four into stanza five. Half-rhymes also help to dampen down the sonic echoing in the poem. The trick is to bend the form so that, despite its rigidity, it can carry the cadences of a spoken voice. Morrissey pulls off this trick with great technical aplomb.

So, now it's the students turn to flesh out the skeleton of Morrissey's poem and then to write their own villanelle on the suggested subject of a school day. By way of encouragement the author has had a go himself and you can find my villanelle at the back of this book. No peeking though, not until you've had a go yourself.

Morrissey's poem sets itself out in a series of declarative statements, seemingly coolly explicating how the narrator has inherited her parents' genes and how these are evident in her body. Hence in some ways, the poem's logic tells us, the parents continue to be married in their daughter. The dominant punctuation mark is the full stop which outnumbers commas. End-stopped lines, emphasised with full stops, give each statement a definite, factual air:

'My body is their marriage register.
I re-enact their wedding with my hands'

This re-enactment even turns back time. When the narrator turns her hands into a church, her mother and father appear as if by magic, 'demure before a priest reciting psalms'. As the poem progresses the repeated refrains of the form work together like rhetorical devices - piling up they insist that reconciliation has taken place.

Why did Morrissey choose the conceit of the hands as a church? I think she made this choice because the 'here is a church, here is a steeple' rhyme is associated with small children. Isn't there something small childish in the poem's wish-fulfilment of reuniting parents who have grown apart? In the poem itself her parents are, indeed, reconciled. But they probably were not in real life. Hence the elegant poem is made poignant through contrast with reality. Why did the poet choose the form of the villanelle to tackle this subject? The form of a villanelle is like a formal dance - lines are rotated, separate and then join back up again. Lines one and three for instance start close, circle each other and finish even closer together as the poem's last two lines. Hence the form embodies the idea of separating and coming back together again; separation and connection between the narrator's parents and between them and her. Perhaps there's even some analogy between the poem's shape and the twists of a genetic code. The narrator is also stuck in the desire to reconcile her parents, a repeating emotional pattern; a need she cannot escape or move beyond. At least not until the final stanza where there's a major shift in the poem.

There is a delayed introduction of an addressee 'you' into *Genetics*. Reading the last stanza, we realise the whole poem has, in fact, been addressed to this silent presence and that the villanelle form is being employed rhetorically, to persuade this person about something important. This much is apparent from the fact that the final stanza begins with a conjunction 'so', a simple synonym for 'therefore'. This is the language of logical argument: A proposition has been advanced, demonstrated and proven and so this final stanza proffers the logical conclusion. The persuasiveness continues with the shift into imperatives. And we realise that *Genetics* is in fact a tender love poem, to the poet's parents, but also to their lover. An offer is made to be with someone and perhaps have a child with them. The tone and manner of the poem might appear cool and sophisticated; a clever conceit is manufactured from a childish rhyme and is elegantly achieved. But underneath this cleverness there's a vulnerability, a sense of loss, a poignant tenderness. And that too is persuasive.

Genetics crunched:

MY – THEM – PARENTS – REPELLED – SEPARATE – TOUCH – NOTHING – IMAGE – LEAST – SHAPE – I – MY – PARENT – MANAGE – SO – FUTURE – BEQUEATH – MAKE

RELATIONSHIPS

Andrew Marvell, *To his Coy Mistress*

It is a truth universally acknowledged that in the most common of all stories [the boy meets girl story] it is the boy who must insist on getting it on. All the while the innocent, naïve and prudish girl must instigate a great strategy of joyless and moral defence. Or so Andrew Marvell [pictured] would have you believe. And who could argue with that face; with that thinly veiled sneer of contempt; with that beautifully manicured moustache? 'His Coy mistress' is the answer to that particular question. She is seemingly oblivious to his various arguments for indulging in sensual/sexual pleasures and has compelled him to vent his frustrations into poetic form instead. What an inconsiderate young wench!

'I'm So Hot For Her and She's So Cold'

The poem is dominated by the male speaker, whose strong subjective persuasion finds its focus on the significant other in the poem: his 'coy mistress'. This crucial adjective tells us much about the relationship itself. The stereotypical active male is laying siege to the defences of the passive female, who fends off his advances through coyness. It epitomizes the age old struggle of seduction, where the wily female must preserve her honour while not alienating the male completely. Commonly associated with coquettish women, this coyness, when viewed from one end of the gender telescope may represent sexual frustration of the most infuriating kind, while viewed from the opposing end it's an essential weapon in ensuring social respectability.

What Marvell cleverly constructs is an oppositional pairing or binary opposite of man – woman; active – passive; subject – object; heat – cold; risk – caution; realistic – idealistic. It smacks of the classic persuasive battles that we would still recognize today but also tells us something about the gender norms of the 17th century. There is a distinct feeling of space and difference and even separation between the speaker and the mistress throughout the poem, especially in the gothic darkness of the second stanza. Conveniently, the logical endpoint of both the poem and the speaker's argument sees the two lovers become one [to utilize an overused pop cliché]. There is no longer a distinct sense of 'You and 'I'; instead it becomes a case of 'Us' and 'We'. The result of such clever transformation from twoness to oneness, from separation to togetherness, is unclear. We never know whether coy becomes joy. Like Marvell, the reader is made to wait as the sensual drama of the poem is never resolved.

To His Coy Mistress is a poem wracked by oppositions. The unity suggested by the 'we' of the first line swiftly broken into a distinct 'I' and 'you'. Throughout the poem a whole series of oppositions emerges that would make structuralists the world over rejoice:

- I vs. you
- Conquest vs. Defence
- Indulgence vs. Denial
- Pleasure vs. Honour
- Present vs. Future
- Life vs. Death

- Male vs. Female
- Excess vs. Scarcity
- Spontaneity vs. Calculated
- Realism vs. Idealism
- Hot vs. Cold

Marvell also constructs another important opposition in the poem: between the speaker and a very abstract entity: Time. Time in various forms is the chassis of Marvell's vehicle for sensual indulgence. It is a vital weapon in the  lascivious logic of the speaker in trying to persuade his mistress to have sex with him. But Time changes shape, so to speak, as the poem progresses. Initially it is an inert thing; as abstract as it really is. However, upon charging into the second stanza Time becomes personified as a heartless predator and thus Time becomes as much of an opponent as the speaker's mistress. In fact the end of the poem becomes more a battle with mortality and the speaker's awareness of the transience of youth and pleasure. In some ways, his apocalyptic persuasive trick of using the tomb has backfired. He has taken his eye off the ball, persuasively speaking, and becomes more obsessed with trying to defy the passage of Time rather than complete his sexual conquest.

The logic of love

The speaker in the poem is confident and strong, full of certainty in his addressing of his lover. The title indicates the poem's modus operandi: it is an appeal to or, maybe even an argument with, a reluctant lover. In the Restoration comedies that dominated the stage of Marvell's later life such male persuasion of guarded female lovers to submit to sensual appetites was rife. However, such antics are not just restricted to Restoration theatre, the battle of the sexes is a universal one. And to put it frankly, the fallout of such struggles remains universal: personal rejection or personal validation through enjoyment. In a time without the benefits of contraception and much more stringent social codes, the problem of illegitimacy was much greater than today. Hence, the struggle between carpe diem & family planning becomes much more violent!

The speaker certainly has a complaint to make: his mistress will not submit to his sexual advances. The poem presents a clever argument that is typical of the metaphysical poets of Marvell's time. The structure of the poem can be summarized succinctly as follows:

IF we had oodles of time → BUT we don't → SO it's loving time!

Clearly it seems a logical, if completely self-serving, structure. The structure of the poem is that of an amorous argument with hypothesis, anti-hypothesis and conclusion and results in a curious combination of rational logic and intimate seduction. Repetition of personal and possessive pronouns indicates the structure of speaker and listener, almost like a dramatic monologue. The auxiliary verb 'would' introduces the hypothetical situation constructed in the first stanza: it has a conditional function, as does the entire first stanza. This helps the speaker to construct the textbook 'if – but – so' argument described above. The verb 'grow' refers to love on one level but also facilitates a descent into sexual innuendo and a certain crude wit. The growth here is most definitely of the erectile variety. An abrupt change of tone is signalled by the verb 'hear' in the opening line of the second stanza, which also signals a sensory change from the predominant visual imagery of the first stanza to the growing importance of aural imagery in the second. It all leads the reader to the tactile overload of the final stanza. The 'think' of the final line in the second stanza also signals the very personal and very subjective nature of the speaker's argument.

Even the length of the stanzas seems to reflect Marvell's mode of argument. The first stanza has 20 lines, which conjures a world where time is in abundance; the second stanza is the shortest, with only 12 lines, reinforcing the counter-argument of time as a non-renewable resource racing towards empty; and finally the last stanza contains 14 lines, which is somewhere between the utopia and dystopia of the previous two stanzas and promotes the idea of enjoying sensual pleasures. The three stanzas also relate to the form of the ode, which is a form that Marvell used for his *An Horatian Ode Upon Cromwell's Return from Ireland*. The function of the ode [long poems involving serious meditations in an elevated style] is highly unsuited to the content and style of this poem. However, the tri-partite structure of the Greek original seems to align with the tri-partite structure of this poem. The strophe, anti-strophe and epode of the Pindaric ode correspond with the hypothesis, anti-hypothesis and conclusion of Marvell's poem. Marvell's ironic use [or abuse] of a serious form connects to his inappropriate harassment of his mistress where he has everything to gain and she has everything to lose.

Opposites attract?

In a poem that relies on building contrast through oppositional states it is no surprise that the imagery follows suit. Given the tonal differences of each stanza it makes sense, for a change, to follow the chronology of the poem.

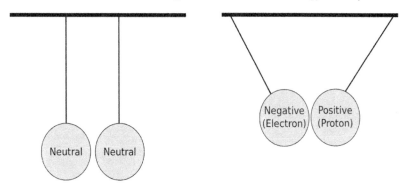

The first stanza is awash with imagery of the infinite, the gigantic. Everything found in the first stanza luxuriates in vastness and abundance. The tone established is one of playfulness and it is hard to take the speaker's words seriously. The hypothetical situation that he creates is one where Time itself is a luxury. This allows the speaker to appreciate his Lady's coyness, but it is also a subtle rejection of such coyness in reality. Marvell builds a contrast between the mistress strolling 'by the Indian Ganges' side' picking rubies. The opposition between seducer and seduced is underscored by the exotic imagery of India, which is juxtaposed abruptly with the more mundane images of the Humber, the estuary of Marvell's hometown of Hull, where the poet languishes. He presents us with a vast spatial contrast as well as a contrast in activities and colour. The Humber is known for its dark waters, which gives an effective contrast with the rubies his lover picks. While he complains, she picks precious stones. It appears to be sly praise, suggesting that his lover deserves such exotic climes due to her own high value. It also neatly equates the female with a beautiful, decorative commodity: the ruby.

The choice of the ruby is also symbolic, where its colour carries connotations of passion and deep sensual energies.

This vastness of space is matched by a vastness of time. When the amorous speaker announces it will take from 'ten years before the Flood … Till the conversion of the Jews' for their seduction to take place he spans from early Biblical times until some far off point in the future. This luxury of time is broken down when the speaker deconstructs his lover's body and dedicates great swathes of time to adoring each. The quick switch from non-sexualized to sexualized parts [i.e. from 'eyes' to 'breast'] signals the seductive rather than courtly motivation of the speaker.

This is also reinforced by the clever sexual innuendo of 'my vegetable love should grow / Vaster than empires'. As we've suggested, the vegetable in question is rather phallic in shape and continues to 'grow' as the male gaze becomes fixated on the sexual parts of  the woman's body. Equating 'love' and 'rate' can be interpreted as purely quantitative i.e. the Lady deserves such gigantic flattery, it is a form of payment to her beauty. More worryingly, love or sex is thus equated with financial terminology, which reflects the financial nature of marriage in this period but also strays into the territory of love as a sort of prostitution. This slyly cynical view observes that sex between man and woman is merely a transaction that is not strictly physical i.e. pleasure for pleasure, rather for the man to obtain sex he must pay with something the woman desires. Possibly the rubies mentioned in the beginning stages? Or just jewelled words.

Time is a hunter

With this hypothetical flattery ringing in his Lady's ears the speaker then takes a sudden jarring change in tonal direction. The second stanza's opening 'But' obliterates the leisurely, sensuous ambling of the previous stanza. Marvell introduces the opposite sensation: Time is hunting them down in its 'winged chariot'. Feelings of persecution are exacerbated by the new barren landscape: the 'Deserts of vast eternity' contrast very strongly with the exotic 'Indian Ganges' and lush 'vegetable love' of the previous stanza. Upping the persuasive intensity, Marvell moves swiftly from utopia to dystopia, from making love to his Lady to the 'marble vault' of her tomb. It's not subtle but it is effective. Marvell moves from abundance of time to scarcity of time in a poetic charge that trails gothic imagery galore in its wake.

The speaker changes tactic: deny me too long and death will have you … and your beauty. Specific details employed by the speaker are shocking: in this scenario, it is the worms not the speaker who will test her defences. The phallic symbolism of the worms as well as the messy equation of death and sex would set any decent Freudian student's heart racing! The patronizing 'quaint honour' described by the speaker is shown to be a needless sham: virgin or not your flesh will be penetrated upon death. To choose a man over a swarm of worms seems to be the obvious and less disgusting choice. Of course, the hypocrisy of a male criticising the very concept imposed upon women by such men as himself points to the sexual double standards of the 17th century. The equation of 'honour' with 'dust' and 'ashes' with 'lust' brings echoes of the funeral service: 'ashes to ashes, dust to dust…' This reinforces the deathly pallor of the stanza in general, and the process of decay in particular, but also universalizes the theme of transience and bodily desire. In this case, death can be equated with aging, i.e. the death of physical beauty. Again, this echoes a very familiar argument: enjoy physicality while you have it, it won't be here forever.

Marvell writes in rhyming couplets, which gives the poem a strong forward momentum. While not technically heroic couplets [rhyming couplets written in iambic pentameter], it could be argued that he writes in unheroic couplets by shaving two syllables off his poetic line. This suits the distinctly unheroic content of the poem, but also gives the poem a swiftness that the heroic couplet cannot instil. He employs a very regular iambic tetrameter throughout the entire poem, a metre also used to great effect in Marvell's The Garden.

> We would / sit down / and think / which way
> To walk / and pass / our long / love's day.

This regular metre reflects the unrelenting nature of the speaker's argument in trying to seduce his mistress but also reflects the universality of this seductive process. There are two notable exceptions to the strict iambic tetrameter metre. In the second stanza, there are 9 syllables in 'Thou by the Indian Ganges' side', which is a way of making it stand out from the mundane familiarity of the 'Humber'. Significantly, the other notable deviation comes early in the decasyllabic 'Time's winged chariot hurrying near'. Here the extra syllables are negated by the narrow vowels in 'chariot' and 'hurrying' so that the line seems to hurry over the extra beat. Here the poem begins its reflection on serious matters: time, mortality, life, death, existence itself. Lovemaking is no longer the only theme. But it is not forgotten either.

The thrill of the chase

With the inescapable logic established by contrasting two extreme states the speaker merely has to spell out the obvious for his Lady: IF only we had time…BUT we don't…SO, let's make the most of it while we can! Now the lovers are assumed to join forces not only for their mutual pleasure but also for their common, and universal, goal of defying Time itself. This final stanza is packed with action verbs: 'sport, 'devour', 'tear', 'run'. The thrill of the chase associated with sexual union has now been enlarged to encompass a larger chase, the thrill of defying Time by packing as much experience into life as possible. The beginning of the stanza establishes a delicate sense of transience, where the 'youthful hue' of his Lady's beauty is about to evaporate. The imagery of 'amorous birds of prey' is another potentially disturbing equation that reinforces relations between men & women as that of predator & prey. The sensual overload of 'devour', 'tear' and 'roll' signals the sensual change from cold tomb to hot bed, from 'echoing song' to tactile heaven. While the image of the 'ball' introduces a sense of strength through togetherness, almost like a hedgehog rolling into a ball to ward off predators. In this case, Time is the predator not the male and the prey is the couple rather than the female. The 'sun' and its gendering as male alludes to classical myth, where Apollo is the sun god who traverses the heavens in a flaming chariot. This personification of the sun, and hence Time itself, turns the contest from gender based to a more universal theme altogether: Mortality itself. The triumphant final couplet preaches carpe diem: seize the moment and take control. Rather than be a passive victim of Time, become Time's master!

Weaknesses of sound, will and flesh

Marvell's rhyming couplets create a sense of certainty in the rhyme scheme though the use of strong, masculine rhyme i.e. 'time' and crime', obviously

reflecting the confidence of the speaker in his argument's persuasive powers. When Marvell uses weaker, slant rhymes they are quite jarring; little sonic snags on the ear. What is more interesting are the words that are emphasized by these slant rhymes: 'lie', 'eternity', 'try' and 'virginity'. In fact these couplets look to be split deliberately; surely 'lie' would be much more suitably paired with 'try' and 'eternity' with 'virginity'. Marvell seems to be playing with these words in a clever but obscure way. Perhaps getting the reader to focus on these four words makes him/her play around with the combinations and come to conclusions that Marvell wants us to consider; maybe that virginity is overrated and is, as such, a lie, or maybe that we should try striving for eternity by cramming our days with as much experience as we can. Maybe the complexity of the words 'virginity' and 'eternity' are the words he wants the reader to ruminate upon as they are complex concepts themselves leading to all types of discussions on love and gender, behavioural norms and time, mortality and decay etc. Ultimately, the weakness in sound patterns also connects to the wider thematic concerns of natural human weakness regarding indulgence of natural desires and also the weakness of the flesh in defying mortality.

The sounds of seduction

In terms of sound patterns Marvell employs assonance in the form of long vowel sounds, especially in the first stanza. This makes sense as the long "O"s of "world enough", "long love", "before the flood" and "more slow" has the effect of slowing the pace. This makes poetic sense as the central idea of the first stanza is to create a scenario where time is not an issue, where the pace is languid. Contrasting with this are the short vowels of the second stanza, particularly the buzzwords of 'eternity' & 'virginity', which quicken the pace and emphasise time is running out. Indeed, the final stanza is a sensual statement that delights in the pleasures of the flesh. Marvell uses sibilance, to create a hissing, sizzling noise that might be appropriate to the hotbed of physical activity that dominates this final stanza:

- 'soul transpires / At every pore with instant fires'
- 'let us sport us […] amorous birds of prey'
- 'sweetness"; our sun / Stand still.'

It may also be a way of creating a sense of deflation, of loss suggesting transience and decay, which ultimately must spur the mistress and the reader to take life by the horns and wrestle for supremacy. Alternatively, this sound could be interpreted more positively; as a background whistling sound that mimics the excitement and swiftness of the chase.

Marvell also uses alliteration in places to add sonic flourishes to his poem. Notably he frontloads and endloads this poem with alliteration, which draws our ear to his hypothetical starting point and the emphatic declaration of the poem's denouement. So in the first four lines he provides alliteration as follows: 'we' and 'world'; 'coy' and 'crime'; 'we', 'would', 'way' and 'walk'; 'long' and 'love'. Proliferation of alliteration adds to the exotic beauty being described in the opening stanza. However, as Marvell progresses into the darker second stanza, all beauty is stripped away to reveal the gothic gloom of the tomb. However, he returns emphatically to alliteration in the final couplet, which adds further emphasis to his message. See the 'th's of 'Thus' and 'though' [which also connect back to the previous line's 'Thorough'], the 'st's of 'Stand' & 'still' & the 'w's of 'we' & 'will'. There is also a notable amount of consonance with "n" & "m" sounds dominating, which give the couplet a lovely soft smoothness to its sound patterns.

To My Coy crunching:

TIME – COYNESS – SIT – LONG – INDIAN – RUBIES – COMPLAIN – FLOOD – REFUSE – CONVERSION – GROW – EMPIRES – PRAISE – EYES – ADORE – THOUSAND – AGE – HEART – DESERVE – RATE – ALWAYS – TIME'S – LIE – ETERNITY – BEAUTY – VAULT – WORMS – VIRGINITY – HONOUR – LUST – GRAVE – EMBRACE – YOUTHFUL – SKIN – WILLING – FIRES – SPORT – AMOROUS – DEVOUR – LANGUISH – ROLL – SWEETNESS – PLEASURES – LIFE – SUN – RUN

Robert Browning, *The Laboratory*

An affair of the heart

Victorian poet Robert Browning is best known for his mastery of the dramatic monologue form and for his marriage to fellow poet, Elizabeth Barrett Browning. Before he was himself famous, Browning fell in love with the already established poet Elizabeth Barrett. But her family barred them from marrying because of Robert's lowly status and relative poverty. Undeterred, the couple eloped to Italy and were duly married. Elizabeth may have been disinherited by her father and cut off from her family, but the two poets seemed to have lived a happy and fulfilling life together.

In canonical poems, such as *My Last Duchess*, *Porphyria's Lover* and, here, in *The Laboratory* the poet takes us into the disturbed minds of psychotic and murderous characters. In some of these great dramatic monologues the speaker's warped state of mind is hidden beneath a veil of elegant language. In *The Laboratory*, however, despite the formal control and external order, the psychosis is always bubbling away vigorously, always threatening to break out and flood the poem's surface.

Inner turmoil

On the surface, the poem looks orderly and well-mannered. There are regular quatrains set out neatly on the page, each completing itself in its final line. Then there is the well-maintained couplet rhyme scheme. Mostly masculine in form, the rhymes are all full and click into place with machined precision. Perhaps this outer order is analogous to the outward appearance of this insanely jealous narrator. After all, she believes she has hidden her malevolence so effectively that the objects of her jealousy think she is in church piously praying when in effect she is in the laboratory watching eagerly as the poison is made.

Only a little closer inspection of the poem reveals her unhinged personality. We don't even have to read the words; just look at the crazy, erratic, urgent punctuation! So many question marks and exclamation marks and so many skittish dashes! Add to that the number of caesuras breaking up the pattern of the verse. Not having to read the words to work this out is analogous to not having to hear the woman speak to recognise the dark disorder of her mind. When we do read the words an obsessive manic quality is immediately apparent. Browning creates this impression through opening the poem with a quadruple rhyme pattern in the first stanza and continues it with repetitive, doubling language, such as 'poison to poison', 'they laugh, laugh at me', and 'know that I know'. More subtlely, the syntax in many lines follows the same or similar pattern, giving the sense of a mind running obsessively down the same narrow lines.

Sadistic relish

The most shockingly disturbing lines are the ones in which the narrator imagines the sadistic pleasure to be gained from carrying her secret, deadly power hidden about her person and when she speaks with such relish about the cowardly murder she hopes to perform. A seemingly powerless, perhaps insignificant woman who describes herself as a 'minion', the narrator thrills to the idea of the 'treasures' of poison that promise a 'wild crowd of invisible pleasures'. Worse, referring to her rival's face she says, 'Brand, burn up, bite into its grace'. Here the tripartite plosive alliteration of the verbs and the growly run of 'r' sounds suggest the speaker's tone. How would you describe this? Bitter and twisted? Snarling and aggressive? Harsh and vindictive? Coolly amused?

From the start Browning positions us as the silent addressee, the 'you' of this brain-fevered monologue, as if we might be the woman's confidant or even her accomplice. Indeed she speaks to us as if we are, in fact, the chemist mixing the poison. Why? What effect does this have do you think? This raises the tricky question of our complicity or at least this silent character's motivation in helping the potential murderer. Browning creates a very distinctive voice for his poisoner. She addresses us in an obsessive, cruel and feverish voice, full of manic urgency and unhinged excitement. Look, for instance, at the number of questions and imperatives and the short, exclamatory phrases that convey her growing impatience: 'Quick—is it finished?'; 'What a drop!'; 'Is it done?' She ends the poem with wild, reckless abandon, offering us/ the chemist everything she has in exchange for her revenge.

Browning, of course, leaves the story before this woman can do her worst.

Too often the only type of response GCSE students are encouraged to write for a poem is the analytical essay. Obviously it is important that they learn how to write essays, but it's healthy to leaven this analytical diet with some more creative tasks, from time to time. Students could continue this poem's narrative, for example, describing what happened at the dance. Their aim would be to maintain the same voice while working in a different form. To maintain the unsettling sense  of intimacy between speaker and reader, a strategy which makes us almost feel complicit with the potential crime, a diary form would suit. Or, if pupils prefer to choose more straightforward narrative, you could discuss the use and function of interior monologue. An effective scene could be created, for instance, with polite, but stilted dialogue between the principal characters interspersed with the narrator's interior monologue of raging malevolence. Using the present tense would add further tension to the piece. The most ambitious students might like to try writing the continuation in verse...

The great show-off, the 'bard of Avon', William Shakespeare was fond of giving his villains soliloquies early in a play. Both Iago and Edmund, for instance, speak the first soliloquies in *Othello* and *King Lear* respectively, and *Richard III* opens the action in the eponymous play. A more modern example from TV of a similar device would be both the British and American versions of *House of Cards*, where the Prime Minister/ President speaks through the camera directly to the audience, as if only he is aware of our presence. Can your students think of any other examples? If you gave them a quick narrative summary, they could read and watch one of Shakespeare's villain's speeches and consider the intended effects on the audience. Are we simply appalled? Does the villain try to get us on their side? Is there a bit of us that wants to see if the villain can succeed with his nasty scheming? Surely not! Do we feel anything similar for Browning's narrator? If not, why not?

 Browning's poem could be the launchpad for an interesting debate on whether female villains are scarier and more disturbing than male ones. Discuss this proposition, sensitively, as a class.

The Laboratory crunch:

I - SMOKES - DEVIL'S - POISON - HER - BELIEVE - LAUGH - PRAY - GRIND - POWDER - THINGS - DANCE - MORTAR - GOLD - EXQUISITE - SWEETLY - TREASURES - PLEASURES - DEATH - FILIGREE - LOZENGE - JUST - PASTILE - DEAD - QUICK - ENTICING - DRINK - TASTE - MINION - ENSNARED - MASCULINE - MAGNIFICENT - THEY - BEAR - FALL - SHRIVELLED - PAIN - FELT - BITE - REMEMBER - DONE - KILLS - FORTUNE - HURTS - GORGE - KISS - HORROR - MOMENT

Elizabeth Barrett Browning, *Sonnet 43*

A modest disguise

Elizabeth Barrett Browning wrote *Sonnet 43* as a private expression of her love for fellow poet Robert Browning, with whom she had begun a secret courtship. The couple later married, but her wealthy father disowned her as he did not approve of her choice. It was only after they eloped and were married that Elizabeth mentioned she had written a series of sonnets about her husband while they were courting. When Robert read them, he thought they were the best sonnets written in English since Shakespeare's and encouraged her to publish. However, they were so personal and revealing, having never been intended for anyone other than Elizabeth Barrett Browning herself, that they were published under the title *Sonnets from the Portuguese*, in an attempt to pretend they were obscure translations of another poet, rather than intimate expressions of her own private emotions. Some of the sonnets, such as *Sonnet 29*, are intensely personal and express a love that is passionate and erotic. *Sonnet 43*, in contrast, conveys a more spiritual, devotional and platonic sort of love. Nevertheless, the reader is given unusually intimate access to the poet's private feelings.

Breadth and depth and height

The short opening question immediately creates a sense of a private conversation, as if the poet is responding to this question. The language is noticeably very simple. In the first line all the words are common monosyllables and they are employed in a literal way within two short sentences that have straightforward syntax. Such simplicity is testament to the honesty and truth of what the poet is saying; there is no need for her to dress up, inflate, disguise or aggrandise her feelings through metaphor or symbolism. Her language is direct, unvarnished and transparent.

In the following lines, however, similarly simple words are used in a more complex, figurative way. Barrett Browning employs a spatial metaphor for the soul and imagines the furthest limits it could stretch - to its utmost 'depth and breadth and height'. Such is the love she feels that it fills her whole soul, reaches even into unknown dimensions ['feelings out of sight'], to furthermost extent of her 'being' and echoes the very best of herself, 'ideal grace'. And this is a poem very much of the soul; the heart, that traditional symbol of love, does not even get a mention. Instead the poem expresses a spiritual, disembodied, idealised love. Hence the religious touchstones of 'grace', 'faith', 'saints' and 'God'.

If this seems impossibly idealistic, rarefied and saintly, Barrett Browning strikes a less elevated note in the following lines. Bringing the poem down to a more ordinary pitch, she refers to the everyday and to what we 'need'. The superlative implies, however, that this not mere clamorous cravings oo desire, but rather the deepest, spiritual needs. The upright, good and virtuous aspect of this love is then developed. The poet associates her love with the universal progressive fight for justice, and praises its resistance to the allurements of ego and vanity. At this point in the poem we have reached the end of the opening eight lines, or octave. Barrett Browning's sonnet follows the Petrarchan form with a rhyme scheme of ABBA ABBA CDC DCD. Technically this is a particularly difficult version of the sonnet to handle in English  because the whole construct has only four rhyme sounds, ABCD. Shakespeare's version of the sonnet, in contrast, almost doubled the number of rhyme sounds to seven, making a Shakespearian sonnet considerably easier to write [though that's only in relative terms, of course]. The fact that Barrett Browning achieves this octave with such grace and apparent lack of effort – the words sound natural despite having to fit such a tight pattern, makes it correlate to the ideal love expressed. The form of the poem not only fits but expresses its meaning. However, a Petrarchan sonnet has a volta in around the ninth line, the first of the sestet. Conventionally sonnets have a call and response or question and answer structure, with the sestet [final six lines] responding to the octave. A volta marks a turn in the subject of a sonnet, sometimes signalled with a 'but' or 'however' or similar signposts for a switch in perspective.

Look for the volta in *Sonnet 43* and you'll not be able to find it. Despite expectations that they must come, no counterarguments to the propositions set out in the octave appear. Instead the poem runs straight over and continues expressing the same loving sentiments, only in new ways. The first line of the sestet, for instance, begins with exactly the same phrase, 'I love thee' as the previous two lines of the octave have done, and overall this simple phrase is repeated four times in both halves of the poem. Hence the whole the depth and breadth and height of the sonnet is filled with ideal love.

After the references to faith, grief and faith, Barrett Browning finishes her sonnet with language that is simple, unadorned and poignant:

'I love thee with the breath/ smiles, tears of all my life'

Moreover, such a love, she tells us, will not only transcend death and become immortal: Perfect though it already is, it will also be refined by death.

The danger with such a restrained and graceful expression of such an elevated, ideal love is that it will feel overly chaste and bloodless; it may seem a love more suitable for angels than for human beings. Though there is a reference to 'passion', this is not the fiery or dangerous passions of erotic or sensual love. Rather it is passion in terms of strong and earnest feelings. There is also a little sense of excited agitation in the lines we quoted above, created by a run of unstressed syllables in both lines and the tripartite list. But perhaps we need to read some of the other sonnets to find the real passion in Barrett Browning's love for Robert. It is surely significant that this poem is the penultimate one in the sequence.

As readers, we are placed in the position of the beloved. We are addressed directly as 'thee' and this rather archaic, perhaps timeless, pronoun is used in almost every line. How would you feel if someone said all this to you? How might Robert have felt? Delighted? Flattered? Daunted? All of these? Perhaps you might like to write his response, in either letter or verse form:

'Dearest Lizzie, I read your poem and I am moved beyond words can express...'

Broadly speaking, historically, sonnets were written most often by men. Frequently they were love poems, often about, and addressed to, women. Women in sonnets tended to objectified, sometimes even deified as goddesses. So the sonnet was a form in which men could show off their wit and write something seductive. Barrett Browning colonises the dominantly male poetic space of the sonnet and demonstrates that she can too handle the form. And that she can do it with just as much panache and variety as any male writer. In this sense, her sonnets can be read from a feminist perspective. Barrett Browning's sonnets equal, or indeed, surpass male artistic achievements in the form [apart from Shakespeare, of course]. In addition, her role as a sonneeter, expressing her love for a male 'object' reflects the loosening of rigid Victorian concepts of gender and the advances made by women towards the end of the age.

Sonnet 43 crunched:

HOW – LOVE – SOUL – IDEAL – EVERY – NEED – FREELY –
PURELY – PASSION – FAITH – LOSE – SAINTS – GOD - BETTER

Christina Rossetti, *Remember*

Rossetti's poem, which opens 'Remember me when I am gone away', is oft-used at funerals. As such it has a cultural identity that aids its effectiveness in stirring sad emotions in us; joining other traditionally used elegies, it presents the speaker from beyond the grave as stoical, selfless and wise. Of course, the poem is spoken by someone living; yet the fact that it is most often used to give a voice to the dead means that it has taken on a different cultural legacy. Its immediate intelligibility lends itself to oral performance. We can hear it once and form a strong sense of its meaning. Rossetti uses very few obvious poetic flourishes or ornamentation; in keeping with the serious material and matter-of-fact tone, the language of *Remember* is unfussily modest and straightforward.

Rossetti was an English poet who belonged to a well-known group of artists and literary figures known as the Pre-Raphaelites. The Pre-Raphaelites sought to return to art as it was composed before or 'pre' the Italian artist Raphael. Specifically they wanted to revive the use of precise detail and intense colour pallets of 15th century Italian art. Christina Rossetti sat for some of the movement's well-known paintings, such as her brother Dante's *The Girlhood of Mary Virgin.*

Rossetti's most famous poem, *Goblin Market,* is full of dark and challenging subversions of the typical children's genre and has proved fertile ground for a host of theoretical excavations from feminists, psychoanalytical readers and Marxists. On the surface at least, *Remember Me* seems a less controversial, more conventional poem.

Remember x 4

The poem uses four 'remember's. The first two set up the command to remember, and the second two quantify these to re-iterate the need for the reader not to forget the speaker of the poem, the person who has died/ will soon die. The first two 'remember's are imperatives, setting the tone for the sentence that will ensue. So is the third; 'and afterwards remember, do not grieve'. However, the last one is in a subordinate clause, linguistically softer, less firm. It is as if Rossetti uses the four markers to take the reader through the journey of grief; from denial and anger in the first part of the poem, with firm, imperative language, to the sadness and acceptance of 'remember' being in the subordinate [or dependent clause].

The first two uses of the word also talk about the future, and the hope of what is lost; the 'silent land' of death is infinite, without the structure of the 'day by day'. Indeed the poem is full of ambiguous time frames - 'a while', 'our future that you plann'd', 'the thoughts that once I had'. Is it as if the speaker is already occupying that space where time has stopped working. The tone of the poem finds its home in a half-existence that is only conjured into being by the implied consciousness of the speaker. The second half of the poem distances itself even further from the present - 'yet if you should forget me for a while / and afterwards remember'. The poem takes us from the first, raw hurt of grief through to future healing in the space a sonnet's fourteen lines - perhaps it is this swift, but restrained outline of the process of grief that leads people to be so emotionally affected by it.

Sometimes saying less, but saying less precisely, can mean more than using lots of looser words. Characteristically Rossetti uses euphemism to underplay the suffering involved in this scenario, including her own. She describes her death, for instance, twice with the casual, everyday phrase, 'gone away'. And death itself is described only as a 'silent land'. The grim reaper is banished from the poem. Absence of the beloved is imagined as no longer being able to hold their hand. The only moment when the chasm of grief begins to open up and threaten to crack the verse's marble-like surface is in the ominous phrase 'darkness and corruption'.

The poem's understated language may be composed predominantly of ordinary words, but their intense patterning is rhetorical. Repetition is a particularly marked feature. Anadipolis sounds like a long extinct dinosaur, but actually it's a term from rhetoric describing ending one line with a phrase and the using it at the start of the next line. Rossetti uses it with 'gone away / Gone far away'. Notice how the addition of the simple word 'far' adds emotional weight to the phrase. Other words and phrases repeated include 'no more', 'should', 'far', 'when' etc. Rhetoric, of course, is appropriate for a poem which seeks to persuade its reader of something. Rossetti's poem counsels the reader not to grieve with sadness. Subtextually, of course, it implies that they/ we must cherish the beloved while we can, before they leave us.

Naturally modern readers do not assume that male poets would be manly and resolute in attitude and matter-of-fact in style. Nor would we think men would especially demonstrate these qualities when facing a subject as grim as their own mortality. If we were tempted to make such gendered assumptions, many of the poems in this anthology would swiftly disabuse us. Equally, we would not expect female poets to be emotional in tone nor florid in expression. Nevertheless it is striking how Rossetti radically reverses Victorian gender stereotypes and it would be interesting to see whether students would gender the poem as male or female if the writer's sex was withheld. *Remember* might not subvert convention as obviously as *Goblin Market*, but it does, in this way, overturn Victorian expectations. Perhaps too the poem's firmly buttoned-down emotion, its stiff-upperlipedness is also an essentially English characteristic. Would the poem be more powerful if Rossetti released her emotions from all this restraint? Would we get something more American and, perhaps, something mawkish?

Going down in good order

What's most striking about this poem is its control. Language is instrumentalised and employed with tremendous precision. There's not a touch of post-structuralist slipperiness to this language or any hint of what T.S. Eliot called the writer's 'intolerable wrestle with words'. Rossetti exerts mastery on her words and through them over her emotions. The management of structural aspects makes this most evident: syllables, the rhyme scheme, lineation, syntax and metre are all kept in good working order. For instance, each line is composed of exactly ten syllables, none are even one more or less. All the rhymes are also full and, despite the stringent technical challenges of the Petrarchan form with its limited number of rhyme sounds, the rhymes slide into place like parts of a well-oiled machine. Each of the first two quatrains is also composed of one sentence that completes itself neatly on the last word of each stanza. This repeated syntactical pattern also neatly brings the poem to the volta, after the octave, and the slight shift of focus in the sestet, signalled by 'yet'.

The metre too is a reliably regular iambic pentameter. Ticking over evenly, it keeps the underlying, potentially destabilising, emotions tucked away. There is only a couple of times when we can hear small disturbances in the poem's even tread. Scan the lines and you'll notice only two slight deviations. The metrical wobbles occur in lines 3 and 12.

The first is a line composed entirely of monosyllables. A regular iambic pentameter would mean that the following syllables are emphasised:

'When **you** can **no** more **hold** me **by** the **hand**'.

Listen to the poem and the emphasis will, however, fall on 'more'. It's simply the more important word in the phrase 'no more' and the line invites a small pause before moving on to the verb 'hold'. Similarly 'me' is surely more important in terms of semantics than the preposition 'by' and thus takes more emphasis. The alliteration of 'm' sounds further foregrounds these two words. The tension here between the poems metrical pattern and its semantic and sonic ones generates this ruffling in the otherwise smooth surface.

In the second example, the regular metre would be: 'A **vestige of** the **thoughts** that **once** I **had**', which would leave a clumsy and unnecessary stress on the small function word 'of'. Again, listen to the line and what we hear is more like 'A **vestige** of the **thoughts** that **once** I **had**'. This is a technique known as pyrrhic substitution, where one stress is diminished, here 'of', so that the following one on 'thoughts' is strengthened. The metrical trailing off and then re-strengthening is highly appropriate to the sense of what is being said. Overall, the extraordinary control of the poem manifests over its material, the exertion of will and reason over destabilising emotions exemplifies, neatly, the poem's overt message to its reader.

How, though, is the reader to feel about being accused, potentially, of forgetting this speaker? Memory is a complicated thing because it calls into question what we call reality, and what we judge as being a real experience. The fact that this poem is culturally used most often to give voice to the dead [prosopopeia] as opposed to giving voice to those about to die means that there is a lack of ability for the reader to reply. Gently it may be, but the poem actually accuses the listener or reader of forgetting someone that they have lost - even the opening line wants to make the reader protest with something along the lines 'Of course I will!' The reader has no right of reply to these accusations, which means that they are left to examine and recognise their own shortcomings in relation to grief and moving on with their lives. There is a silence where there should be correspondence, or a counter-argument.

Because the reader has no opportunity to say that they will, of course, remember the person who has passed away, there is a double sadness to which people react: the sadness of the death and the guilt that they might one day fulfil the accusation of the poem. Narrative silences are really important in literature because they indicate an inability to respond, and a conspicuous gap where there would otherwise be someone controlling the narrative. Interestingly, here it is the person who is either dead, or about to die, who has the voice; the person still living is made silent.

Do you think the poem would be more or less effective if it were a dialogue between two specified people?

Afterlife

The afterlife isn't exactly a bustling party here, or a vision of Bacchus handing out the wine on Mount Olympus. It's an euphemistically phrased 'silent land' which has none of the 'future that you plann'd'. Worse, as we've noted, it's full of 'darkness and corruption'. This is a living person describing the grave, not a voice describing heaven. It's interesting to point out that Rossetti rejected a fiancé because he turned back to the Catholic church; she began to become interested in the Anglo-catholic Oxford movement, becoming a woman of religious devotion. Five years before *Remember Me* was written [1862] she had had a religious crisis. It's striking, therefore, that death in this poem doesn't lead to resurrection in the life beyond. This could have been a point of consolation – I will be dead but will live on eternally in heaven – but this is not what Rossetti wishes to emphasise. Whilst the 'silent land' could at a stretch indicate the heaven of eternal rest [as put forth in the New Testament] it is a curious turn of phrase - to describe heaven as a sterile and 'dark' place is theologically dubious at best. It seems more likely that as a non-devotional poem, this work addresses the very real, frequent and everyday way of coping with the enormously high death rate in Victorian Britain. It has the tone of a didactic tale on how to cope with death.

There's an interesting dynamic in the fact that the speaker here effectively writes their own elegy. It's important to be aware of how we perceive control over a literary narrative - but even more here, the person about to die is trying to guide the memories that other people have of them, which form a sort of afterlife in themselves. It also creates and maintains the exact life after death which the speaker is arguing perhaps doesn't exist in the 'silent land'. Whenever the poem is read or spoken, this idea is continually recalled and comes to symbolise much bigger ideas of loss, grief and pain through Rossetti's unspecific and ambiguous terminology. She does not tie her speaker down to a time or a place; the lack of response from another voice means that the poem comes to represent all those who have passed away, and the slow transition of time that ensures an afterlife in memory, as well as a general fading of conscience.

Form and allusion

It's in the classic form of a Petrarchan sonnet, often used in poems where the subject is unrequited love. Normally, however, it is the speaker of the poem that is suffering from unrequited love; here it is the reader.

An allusion to the tale of Orpheus and Eurydice can be found in the line 'nor I half turn to go yet turning stay'. Orpheus, after the death of his beloved Eurydice, goes down to Hades to ask for Eurydice back. Hades tells him that

he can take her back to the living world on one condition; that on walking out of the Underworld, he should not look back at her, but instead carry on walking lest she be lost for ever. Obviously [because these things don't have happy endings] he turns around to see her because he lacks faith in what the gods have told him. The speaker of the poem wants the reader to have faith that they should be separated, and it is right and proper that this should happen; to chase the person who has died into the 'silent land', or Hades, is not what has been intended by fate. The same 'turning back' can also be found in the sestet, where the speaker describes 'Yet if you should forget me for a while / And afterwards remember, do not grieve'; it is implied that one turns back to grief as one turns back to a memory of a loved one.

Remember Me crunched:

REMEMBER – GONE – SILENT – HAND – STAY – REMEMBER – FUTURE – PRAY – FORGET – GRIEVE – DARKNESS – CORRUPTION – THOUGHTS – FORGET – SMILE – REMEMBER – SAD

Philip Larkin, *Wild Oats*

What does the phrase 'sowing your wild oats' mean? It's an expression that conjures up images of youthful excess, a carefree recklessness about sexual relationships before settling down to the responsibilities of marriage and parenthood. It's therefore an ironic title for Philip Larkin's poem about his relationship with Ruth Bowman, the schoolgirl he met whilst working as a librarian in Wellington, Shropshire, in 1943 – a relationship that, so far as the poem goes, seems to have been neither reckless nor particularly pleasurable. [In later life, Bowman remembered Larkin as being 'relaxed and cheerful, entertaining and considerate', a description of him that is particularly unexpected considering the poet's Eeyorish reputation]. Taken as a whole, this is a poem about disappointment and disillusionment, about a relationship that seems from the start to have been marked by Larkin's sense of his own inadequacy.

Life stories

As *Wild Oats* is an autobiographical poem, let's sketch in a few facts. When Larkin and Bowman met, he was 21 and she was 16. According to James Booth, who has written widely on Larkin, Bowman was 'a real, serious-minded schoolgirl' who was 'dazzled' by Larkin, the Oxford graduate and aspiring poet who had ended up in her small Shropshire town in his first job after leaving university. They read poetry to each other and Bowman stole a copy of Yeats' poems from her school library to give to Larkin. In May 1948, they became engaged. Their relationship ended in September 1950, when Bowman wrote to Larkin to break off their engagement, just as he was moving to Belfast to take up a new post as sub-librarian at The Queen's University. [By this time – and unbeknown to Bowman – Larkin had already embarked on the long-term relationship with Monica Jones, lecturer in English at Leicester University, that was to last until his death in December 1985]. Shortly after he first met Bowman, Larkin described her in a letter to his friend Jim Sutton as 'the only girl I have met who doesn't instantly frighten me away'. Yet in *Wild Oats*, there's none of this warmth and companionship. Instead, Bowman is presented as a compromise, the less attractive of the two girls – a prime example of the gap 'between what Larkin expects of love and what it provides' that has been identified by Andrew Motion as one of Larkin's most persistently-explored topics.

The narrator's colloquial, confiding voice is established right from the first  line of *Wild Oats*, with the casual 'About twenty years ago' [the poem was written in 1962, so the events described in the poem actually took place nineteen years previously]. The poem records Larkin's first meeting with Bowman, when she was accompanied by her friend Jane Exall. Significantly, it's Exall who features first, sketched in a few caricatured details as a 'bosomy English rose' while Bowman is 'the friend in specs I could talk to'. This cartoonish pair represent two stereotyped opposites – one beautiful, sexualised and unattainable - the other unattractive but more approachable. The American wit and writer Dorothy Parker, famous for her pithy wisecracks, once commented that 'men seldom make passes at girls who wear glasses', but clearly for Larkin – himself so short-sighted that he was deemed unfit for military service during the Second World War – the 'friend in specs' was the safer bet. Notice that relationships here are depicted as a kind of trial, a rite of passage that's definitely less than pleasant. The idiom Larkin uses is 'the whole shooting-match' – a phrase that carries overtones of conflict and competition, and also suggests that relationships are something of a chore. He is clearly out of his league – an idiom that he doesn't use, but could have – with the 'bosomy English rose' and therefore settles for second best, underlined by his use of end-focus as the first stanza reaches its conclusion. The impersonality of 'the friend' is telling: Bowman is defined by her relationship to Exall, rather than being a person in her own right.

A little less conversation

The most significant aspect of the relationship between Larkin and Bowman is the way that Larkin depicts it in terms of quantities and transactions, rather than emotions. Look how many references there are to numbers: 'about twenty years'; 'two girls'; 'seven years after that'; 'over four hundred letters'; 'gave a ten-guinea ring'; 'numerous cathedral cities'; 'I met beautiful twice'; 'about five attempts'; 'two snaps'. It's as if Larkin has kept a tally of what he has done and how much he has spent during the years he and Bowman were together. His focus is firmly on what *he* has done: he took her out, wrote her letters and gave her a ring. You can almost imagine him calculating what he must be owed in return. We imagine, perhaps, that he hope he's earnt some wild oats. If this makes Larkin seem resentful and miserly, then this is clearly a deliberate ploy, because he's not afraid to draw attention to his own inadequacy. There's a clear example of this at the end of the second stanza, when we're reminded that the 'bosomy rose' is not a fantasy figure glimpsed from afar, but a real presence who is therefore able to make Larkin perfectly aware of what she thinks of him. Larkin's statement that 'I believe / I met beautiful twice' is both succinct and brilliantly expressive, its mock-casual 'I believe' balanced by the dryness of 'beautiful'. Her mocking rejection of Larkin – 'She was trying / Both times [so I thought] not to laugh' – underlines his awareness that in her eyes, he is a faintly ridiculous figure. Poor Larkin: not only does *he* know that he isn't good enough for 'bosomy rose', but she does as well, and he knows that she does. If *Wild Oats* is a self-portrait, it's one that looks the poet's failings right in the eye.

Indeed, one of the saving charms of this most unromantic of love poems, emptied entirely as it is of the sometimes florid language of love, is Larkin's unflinchingly unromantic depiction of himself as a lover. He's nothing like a Romantic literary hero, such as Lord Byron, pictured opposite, or like a suave matinee idol of the time, such as Frank Sinatra. Larkin does not try to present himself as dashing or charming or handsome, or even witty. In fact, he's distinctly

ordinary, humdrum and rather blokeish [he seems fixated on the rose's 'bosomy' charms]. The poet does not employ any sort of soft or flattering light; we feel he is being, in fact, honest about himself and his relationships. This is the honest, down-to-earth, sceptical Larkin that his friend Kingsley Amis described as demonstrating 'the scrupulous awareness of a man who refuses to be taken in by inflated notions of either art or life'. In this poem, Larkin, or his persona, refuses to be taken in by inflated or sugar-coated ideas about love and relationships.

The fact that he still remembers this meeting, from 'twenty' years back, and sees it as significant still, suggests this was the closest he ever actually got to 'sowing his wild oats', which could be seen as tragic or comic, or both. Perhaps there is a certain wry humour to the self-deprecating way Larkin depicts himself; in public the poet did seem to enjoy presenting himself as a rather glum, Eeyorish figure. Larkin excelled especially at writing about stunted, unfulfilled lives, about characters who feel awkward and inadequate, including himself.

There's more inadequacy, for example, in the final stanza, which details the end of Larkin and Bowman's relationship. The poet depicts himself as entirely passive in this break-up, portraying it as a dispassionate, one-sided 'agreement / That I was too selfish, withdrawn / And easily bored to love'. Notice that he simply counters this judgement with a sour agreement that's also a dismissal: 'Well, useful to get that learnt'. There's a sense, really, that he knew this all along. [Larkin seems remarkably faithful to the truth here. When Bowman wrote to Larkin to end their relationship, she alluded to the sense of dissatisfaction and discontent that had clearly marked Larkin's behaviour: 'I hope that you will be happy in Ireland and that you will, in a new environment, be able to come to better terms with life and with yourself'.]

There's a final sting. At the end of the poem, the narrator reveals that 'In my wallet are still two snaps / Of bosomy rose with fur gloves on'. These photographs – described by Andrew Swarbrick as 'the contraband of fantasy smuggled into the real world' – underline the gap between the unattainable and the reality, between what one would like and what one has to settle for. The poem's final line – 'Unlucky charms, perhaps' – is perhaps an admission that clinging to this fantasy blighted the poet's relationship with Bowman or other women more generally, that it's best to be happy with what you've got rather than hanker after something else. But the final hedge, 'perhaps' – a statement and not a question – suggests that if they *have* been unlucky charms, then Larkin doesn't really care.

Wild Oats crunchy:

YEARS – GIRLS – BOSOMY – SPECS – SPARKED – SHOOTING-MATCH – EVER – BUT – SEVEN – LETTERS – RING – END – NUMEROUS – BELIEVE – BEAUTIFUL – LAUGH – PARTING – AGREEMENT – SELFISH – BORED – USEFUL – WALLET – ROSE – PERHAPS

Carol Ann Duffy, *Before You Were Mine*

Sometimes when we're short of time and preparing pupils for exams which focus on analytical readings of literature we can neglect more creative ways into a text. Duffy's poem lends itself readily to creative approaches. For instance, set a class a creative piece of writing based on the poem. Specifically, pupils should find some old photographs of relatives of theirs [it doesn't have to be their mother and probably will work better with a grandparent or great aunt or uncle] picking three or four as their main focus. They should then think of a memory they associate with this person and a couple of objects with special significance, what Duffy calls 'relics'. Their task then is to write at least a couple of paragraphs describing this person and their feelings about them, both positive and negative. As this is potentially a revealing, personal experience, I'd recommend you only mark the work if pupils would like you to.

The piece justifies itself as descriptive and reflective writing, but it can also be used to illuminate Duffy's poem and to help pupils write about an aspect of poetry they often find challenging – the impact of form and structure. For instance, though it's arranged on the page in neatish looking stanzas, *Before You Were Mine* doesn't have either a regular metre or a rhyme scheme. Whisper it about a poem by the poet laureate if you dare, but is this poem really prose just chopped up and arranged neatly to look like a poem? What might save it from such an accusation? Well, the poem would have to have clear benefits from the way it has been arranged on the page. In other words, the lineation and stanza form must actively contribute to its effects, otherwise it really is just prose disguised to look like poetry. A great, active way for pupils to investigate the significance of form is to present it first to them as prose and to set them the task of arranging it into whatever lines and stanzas they think would work best. To break the task down a little, they could read the first couple of stanzas, re-arranged as prose, as shown below. Their task is then try to package the words back into a first stanza. Once they've had a go, swap examples, show them Duffy's choice and then challenge them to predict the shape of the subsequent stanzas.

Before You Were Mine's first two stanzas prosefied:

I'm ten years away from the corner you laugh on with your pals, Maggie McGeeney and Jean Duff. The three of you bend from the waist, holding each other, or your knees, and shriek at the pavement. Your polka-dot dress blows round your legs. Marilyn. I'm not here yet. The thought of me doesn't occur in the ballroom with the thousand eyes, the fizzy, movie tomorrows the right walk home could bring. I knew you would dance like that. Before you were mine, your Ma stands at the close with a hiding for the late one. You reckon it's worth it.

This task foregrounds the issue of regularity. What might be gained, for instance, by varying the number of lines in the second stanza? And what is, in fact, gained by Duffy's arrangement? Which words gain a little bit of extra stress by the way they are placed on the page? Where does Duffy use enjambment to link across lines and where does she use caesura to break lines and sentences up. Now when you show the class the whole poem they are more likely to be keyed into aspects of form, more likely to notice the consistency of the stanza pattern and already be engaged in thinking about its effect and significance.

If they're not used to this sort of task, your students might find it helpful be given some examples of how the sentences could be possibly be arranged in poetic form:

Arrangement #1; Duffy dons her Emily Dickinson disguise:

I'm ten years away from the corner
you laugh on with your pals -

Maggie McGeeney and Jean Duff -
The three of you bend from the waist

holding each other, or your knees -
and shriek at the pavement.

Your polka-dot dress blows round -
your legs - Marilyn. I'm not here yet.

The thought of me doesn't occur -
in the ballroom with the thousand eyes.

Arrangement #2; Duffy does concrete poetry:

                    I'm
              ten years
         away from the corner you laugh
on with your pals, Maggie McGeeney
and Jean Duff. The three of

              you bend

       from the waist
,holding each

other,   or your knees,
and   shriek   at the pavement.
  Your polka-dot dress   blows   round

              your legs.
              Marilyn.
              I'm not here
                    yet.

With these possibilities in mind, let's consider Duffy choices of lineation. The most obvious benefit the poet gains from her arrangement of the poem into five line stanzas [cinquains] is a sense of order and control. Each of the images, all the memories, the poet's or persona's* feelings, those of her mother, her friends, her clothes and so forth are all boxed and contained within robust-looking stanza frames. The fact that each of these frames is five lines long is a signal that unbroken, unchanging order has been imposed on the unruly, hazy stuff of memory. This impression is enhanced by the fact that each stanza is also complete unto itself; each one ending with either an emphatic full stop or a question mark.

* We'll come back to the question of the identity of the speaker later in the essay, for efficiency, for now, we'll refer to them as the poet.

Duffy's lineation also makes the full stops more obvious and pronounced. There are four of them in just the first stanza all appearing at the end of lines. In the first case, after 'on' they allow the reader a moment to reflect on the potential significance of the opening two lines. The double full stops in the last line, after both 'legs' and 'Marilyn' help create a sense of separate snapshots of the mother the poet is stringing together into a narrative. That last word is also, of course, an incomplete or truncated sentence. So, if the stanza form of the poem signals order, here we have the opposite, the rules of syntax breaking down. Finally, the lineation also allows Duffy to give important words a bit more of a push than they would have in a prose version. The most significant example is that final word, 'Marilyn', stuck on its own, isolated at the end of the stanza.

As we have noted, the stanza form gives the impression of neat, controlled order imposed on the material and, in particular, on its subject, the mother, while other elements run counter to this pattern. As well as the syntax, there is a lack of a regular metre. There is no set number of beats per line and the lines also have different numbers of syllables, ranging in the whole poem from the shortest [10] to the longest [17]. There is something about this material, it seems, that resists the attempt to box and trim it into shape. Tonally, too, the poem is uncertain, difficult to pin down. The opening images of the mother and her friends depict them in an uncomplicated way, having fun together. But these images are preceded and shadowed by the poet's presence 'I'm ten years away'. And isn't there something a little creepy and unnerving about the poet's unseen presence, silently watching her oblivious mother's carefree behaviour? Something rather voyeuristic? Something a little like a security camera? And though the comparison of the mother with the glamorous actress Marilyn Monroe might at first appear to be flattering, Monroe was a famously troubled sex symbol who committed suicide. The poet doesn't divulge clues as to her feelings so we don't know how to take that stark label 'Marilyn'. Could the tone, in fact, be accusatory or envious?

Sweethearts

Certainly, the mother is presented in other ways that also connote glamour as well as energy and self-confidence. Her clothes, for instance, such as the 'polka-dot dress' and her 'high-heeled red shoes'. She is a 'bold girl',

'winking', attending dances at ballrooms, having fun with her mates, unabashed. Her life seems full of promise of a bright future, 'fizzy movie tomorrows'. The adjective here suggests fun, childhood and ebullience and is echoed in 'sparkle', while the reference to 'movies' accords with the image of Monroe. The fact that the ballroom has a 'thousand eyes' and the mother has 'small bites on her neck' imply popularity and romance. As does the word 'sweetheart'. But this affectionate noun is not employed in the poem by a potential lover, but transgressively and unnervingly by the poet narrator. This implies she has feelings towards the mother more usually associated with those of a lover. In this light, other images, such as the 'lovebites' suggest an edgy jealousy, particularly as this image is couched as a question 'whose small bites?'

Mine, mine, mine

We mentioned earlier that Duffy's poem could be read either broadly autobiographically, expressing the poet's feelings about her mother, or if we take the narrator to be a persona, it could be read as a dramatic monologue. Either way, the narrator of the poem, seeing but unseen, is a rather unsettling, ominous, even threatening presence. There's something egocentric, for example, about the way they top and tail the poem with themselves ['I'm'; 'mine'], as if everything, including their mother's life before they were born, now starts and ends with them. Then there's the repeated, possessive phrase 'before you were mine', and its echo in 'I wanted'. Add to that the unnerving phrases we have already noted and others, such as calling the mother a 'ghost' as if she is dead already, or 'I see you, clear as scent', which could either innocently suggest perfume or more disturbingly the scent of an animal being tracked and hunted. Think of how the latter might tie in with the overall sense of invisible surveillance. Then there's the implication of the poem's final sentence, 'that glamorous love lasts / where you sparkle and waltz and laugh before you were mine'; surely all the fun and freedom is over now. Consider too the very firm imposition of control and order and we arrive, perhaps, at something close to the sort of pathological jealousy we saw in Browning's *Porphyria's Lover*. Or are we being too melodramatic? Is Duffy just being honest about how having a child can affect a parent's, and specifically a mother's, life and about how possessively a child's love for their mother can be? We'll leave that up to you to decide.

Before you were Mine crunched:

I'M – PALS – THREE – SHRIEK – MARILYN – YET – TOMORROWS – I – BEFORE – WORTH – YELL – RELICS – GHOST – SCENT – BITES – HOME – WRONG – WANTED – LASTS – MINE

Tony Harrison, *Long Distance II*

Father & son

This moving and powerful poem is taken from a collection called *The School of Eloquence* in which Harrison reflects upon his relationship with his parents and especially explores the distance that opened up between the poet's working class father and the educated literary figure of the poet. The second in a pair of poems focusing on the poet's father, *Long Distance* explores both father's and son's painful difficulties coping with the death of Harrison's mother.

The first half of the pair of poems is written predominantly from the father's perspective and in his voice. The father's forthright speech patterns and Yorkshire accent are rendered using phonetically spelt English. For example, 'Ah've allus liked things sweet! But now ah push/ food down mi' throat! Ah'd sooner do wi'out.' Indeed issues of language, class and power inform all of Harrison's work, with the poet intensely alert to the social snobbery, including his own, that is often revealed in attitudes to dialect and accent. In an earlier poem in the collection, *Book Ends II*, for instance, father and son argue over the inscription to go on the gravestone and the poet passes the following harsh judgement on his father's proposed wording, 'mis-spelt, mawkish, stylistically appalling'. But he then goes on to admit, more tenderly, 'but I can't squeeze more love into' the stone.

Though he's writing in verse, Harrison employs unfancy, ordinary language, heightened but close to the patterns of speech. Indeed in some poems, as we've already indicated, he includes passages of direct speech. We don't find any fantastical metaphors or extravagant phrasing in Long Distance. Whereas the fact that he is writing and writing poetry distances Harrison from his parents, the grounded, down-to-earth language brings them closer together.

Distance & closeness

The title of the poem refers to long distance phone calls, i.e. calls to places a long way away, a reference that is picked up in the last stanza. Clearly there is a number of long distances in the poem: There is distance in time - it has been two years since the mother has died; the emotional distance between father and son and the ultimate long distance between the living and the dead. There is another sense of long distance too; an  implication that the father's recovery will take a long time, that it will be a sort of marathon or endurance race as he goes through the various painful stages of grief and mourning.

In contrast to these long distances, the language of the poem and its images are intimate, tender and domestic. Images such as the 'slippers warming by the gas' and the 'hot water bottles her side of the bed' take us inside the father's private world and lay bare the small kindnesses loving couples do for each other. And, of course, very poignantly these images reveal the father's inability to come to terms with his wife's death. Though two years have elapsed, his love is 'still raw', like an open wound. Later the sonic imagery of the key ['scrape'] and the fact that the lock is 'rusted' add to the sense of his rawness and pain. [Notice how the poet emphasises 'scrape' through placing it at the start of the line and by reversing the metrical foot to a trochee so that we hit it a bit harder.] Yet, in the second stanza, it seems the father is in some ways and to some extent aware of what he is doing. Clearing away 'her things' in order to 'look alone', he is ashamed that privately he needs to keep up the pretence that his wife is still alive. In some ways he is perhaps keeping her alive in his mind by going through these familiar, tender routines and warding off acute loneliness. On the other hand, at other times, it appears the father does really believe his wife might just be temporarily absent and will be coming back soon, 'He *knew* she'd just popped out to get the tea'.

The poet observes his father's worrying, traumatised behaviour and understands just how vulnerable he is. Harrison must have wanted to address his father's behaviour and to try to help him to move on in some way. But the poet is very aware of the potentially destructive impact of any intervention he might make. The metaphor he uses, for example, is 'blight of disbelief', which implies the potential complete devastation of the father's delicate state of mind and ability to cope.

In the last stanza Harrison switches his attention away from his father to his own reaction to his mother's death. The first declarative line seems almost blunt - a cold, matter-of-fact rationalist statement that could be read as a harsh corrective to his father's emotionally-driven behaviour:

'I believe life ends with death, and that is all'

But then, in a surprising turn of events, the poet admits that he still writes 'your name' in his new phone book and even tries to call the 'disconnected number'. So, in the final stanza of the poem the distance between son and his father collapses. Despite being able to recognise the irrationality of his father's behaviour, despite being able to understand that the father is struggling to cope with the reality of his wife's death, the poet finds himself doing something very similar after his father has died. Elsewhere in this collection of poems the mother, when still alive, upbraids her son and husband for sitting apart, not talking to each other, calling them a pair of 'bookends' on a shelf, an image that perfectly captures the separation between them but also their fundamental similarity.

An expanded sonnet

Like many of the poems in *Songs of Eloquence*, *Long Distance* is composed in an extended sonnet form. The sonnet is, of course, commonly associated with love poems, especially poems written to or about a lover. Whatever the content of the poem might express, and in some of these poems Harrison makes frank and unsentimental comments both about his father and about their often abrasive relationship with each other, the holding form of the sonnet signals underlying, enduring, resolute love. The form also provides a comforting regularity within which difficult raw emotion is expressed and contained. For instance, each stanza of this poem ends with a sonically satisfying full rhyme and an emphatic full stop, while, with just a few exceptions, the iambic pentameter keeps the sonnet's engine ticking over smoothly.

Harrison employs a cross-rhyme scheme in the first three stanzas of the poem, but shifts to envelope rhyme in the fourth and final one. The shift neatly emphasises the change in focus of this stanza and, with its internal rhymed couplet, the envelope pattern suits the more introspective nature of these final lines.

Father, I and you

The pronouns in Harrison's poem are interesting and revealing. Having initially referred to his father using the intimate, personal word, 'dad', from then on the poet uses the pronouns 'he' and 'his'. What difference would it make if the poem were addressed to the father? As in '*you* kept her slippers' and '*your* still raw love' and so forth? Using the third person creates a little emotional distance, whereas second person would bring poet and father closer as if in conversation. When the second person is used in 'you couldn't just drop in' it contributes to the running tension in the poem between closeness and distance. The pronoun includes us, bringing us closer to the experience, but on the other hand, it creates distance for the poet. Compare, for example, the rawer alternative, '*I* couldn't just drop in. *I* had to phone'. Withholding this first person pronoun until the last stanza almost makes its introduction more marked and emphatic. Notice too, how in this stanza 'you' is used again, but in a different way. Here it refers to Harrison's mother and father, 'you haven't both gone shopping'. The last use of the pronoun in 'your name' is ambiguous - it could refer to the father or to both mother and father. Subtlely, at the end of the poem, Harrison addresses his father directly and more personally, as if he needed to build-up to this tender moment. Subtlely too he lets readers infer that now the father has also died, and the poet is bereft.

Long Distance crunched:

MOTHER - WARMING - BED - RENEW - COULDN'T - TIME - LOOK - RAW - BLIGHT - SURE - SCRAPE - KNEW - DEATH - HAVEN'T - NEW - STILL

CONFLICT

Alfred Lord Tennyson, *The Charge of the Light Brigade*

Us vs. them

For a poem so stuffed with soldiers and horses and cannons, there is a rather faceless quality to the entire affair. Tennyson creates the sterile stereotypes that are necessary in all conflicts: Us and Them. The doomed brilliance of the British army is captured by the 'noble six hundred', who seem to act as one entity.

The British soldiers embody the type of bravery that resulted in the largest empire since ancient Rome. Not only are they courageous and 'noble' but they are unquestioning too: 'Theirs not to reason why.' We must remember that in Tennyson's day, such unquestioning obedience was to be praised. After the twentieth century's world wars and Vietnam, and with changing conceptions of the afterlife, such automatic and unquestioning obedience may be seen as foolish nowadays.

repetition and anaphora

The Light Brigade epitomize speed, action and courage. Even their physical position, on horseback, elevates them symbolically above their enemies. They are also associated with light in terms of God and goodness, with Tennyson here playing on their military classification. Such positive connotations are continued in the use of the verb 'flashed' as the Light Brigade engage with the opposition. This association with light is slyly associated with right as they beam through the gloom of the 'battery-smoke'.

metaphor from the Bible

Waiting for them at the other end of the 'valley of Death' lie the enemy: the Russians and Cossacks. In contrast to the dynamic movement of the Light Brigade, they simply sit and wait, plotting the downfall of their noble adversaries. Even their weapon of choice tells us something of their dubious personalities: cannons versus sabres. Surely no contest? Unfortunately, for them their smugness is about to be 'shattered and sundered by the rapid romantic sabres of the Light Brigade. The important verb 'reeled' suggests enemy weakness in the face of overwhelming valour, despite the disastrous reality of the situation. This discrepancy between the two fighting groups magnifies the feats of the Light Brigade whilst simultaneously belittling the fighting prowess of the Russians. Tennyson seems to be saying 'Go Britannia'! even when the British are going in the wrong direction to almost certain death!

There is also another group which we must consider; a group who are responsible for the event, but not for the bravery. The commands of Lord Raglan create the opportunity for British fighting men to shine when confronted by high danger. However, how should we respond to the crucial verb 'blundered'? We are now firmly located in that age-old wartime debate about who commands and who fights and, more importantly, who gets the glory of martial success. Such debates stretch back as far as Homer's Iliad, where Achilles gets put out by his commander's [Agamemnon] demands for the spoils of war. We remember Nelson and Churchill, but who were the brave souls who actually did the fighting? And that is partly the problem. For a more modern take on this tension between commanders and commanded, we need to look forward to the poetry of Siegfried Sassoon and Wilfred Owen.

Let there be [no] blood

You don't need a Degree in English Literature to recognize the dominance of war imagery in the poem, but what is striking is the distinct lack of violence. Saving Private Ryan it is not! This is poetry written in an age preoccupied with moral decency and glory; blood splattered poetry would horrify rather than rouse Tennyson's reading public. Tennyson instead creates a very dramatic, almost cinematic, poem that focuses on movement. The driving force of the Brigade itself hurtles the reader into the midst of the battle, where Tennyson surrounds us with the sounds of war as opposed to the sights. A real sense of forward momentum is generated by:

uses sounds instead of sounds

- verbs like 'charge'
- the quasi-onomatopoeic 'plunged'
- the metre
- the short line lengths

The first image of note is one where Tennyson makes it clear that this is not just some propagandist vehicle hurrahing the might of the British Military. When he proclaims that the Light Brigade are charging across 'the valley of Death' we are left in no uncertain terms that destruction and loss is inevitable. In one way, of course, this makes the feat of the Light Brigade even more awe-inspiring [or stupid]. The valley of Death delivers a clear biblical clang for Tennyson's Victorian audience as it borrows from Psalm 23: 'Yea, though I walk through the valley of the shadow of death, I will fear no evil: for thou art with me; thy rod and thy staff they comfort me'. This imaginatively captures the physical space of the battle i.e. a valley but also manages to foreshadow the massive losses suffered by the Light Brigade.

The valley of death becomes almost a motif that Tennyson uses throughout the poem, sometimes with interesting variations. The valley of death is repeated in stanza two and in stanza three is developed by linking death with hell itself. The valley of death becomes 'the jaws of death', which personifies death as an all-consuming monster. Tennyson cleverly links the 'jaws' to the 'mouth', but the mouth now belongs to hell rather than death itself. The gothic imagery suggests that the Light Brigade are food for the war machine. Again, this particular coupling of 'jaws of Death' and 'mouth of hell' appears in the fifth stanza. This time, though, the Light Brigade retreat back rather than charge into the terrible site of violence.

Auditory imagery, associated with the cannons that pepper the charging cavalry, is particularly powerful. The fact that cannons lined both sides of the valley, as well as awaited them at the valley's end, meant that the Light Brigade were showered with deadly explosives from all angles. The booming cannons are captured through:

- The mere repetition of the word itself. The repetition of 'cannon' at the start of stanza three mimics the sequential firing of the cannons.

- Repetition is employed again in the fifth stanza where the Light Brigade must face the firing cannons for the second time.

- Tennyson employs storm imagery to capture the reality of the battlefield where he uses the verb 'thundered'. This evokes not only the sound of the cannons but also strengthens the foreshadowing that all hell is about to break loose.

- Tennyson stretches this imagery by using another related verb: 'stormed': The 'shot and shell' from the cannons rains down on them in a storm of fire.

This fourth stanza also contains possibly the most important visual image in the poem: that of the Light Brigade's bright sabres. Another example of repetition, the key word in the opening couplet is '<u>Flashed</u>'. The brightness of the metal sabres carries a positivity that contrasts with the dark cannons. It also intensifies the drama of Tennyson's cinematic treatment - the gleaming blades slicing through the oppressive enemy smoke. By using the hand held light sabres it elevates the British soldiers above their enemies.

This is interesting imagery itself: These verbs don't seem to suit actions suffered by humans, but rather damage made to a faceless machine. Again, it is more difficult to sympathise with enemy robots being dismantled than seeing fellow human beings brutally sliced and diced in your name.

A strategy of repetition

As in many poems, repetition is a key device in *The Charge of the Light Brigade*. The first example of the strategy of repetition is at the very start: 'Half a league, half a league, / Half a league onward'. The caesura right in the middle of the opening line creates a sense of balance before the onward thrust of the second line. Repetition of 'half a league' also allows the narrator to present the point of view of the cavalrymen. There is no doubt as to whose side we are to be on. It also creates suspense; the moment of engagement must be waited for, by both Light Brigade and reader. The first line also mimics the galloping of the charging horses in its sound effects [try it yourself and see what rhythm you construct]. This metre never relents, which further adds to the poem's forward momentum.

Tennyson also uses what might be termed a refrain, or a repeated section, at the end of each stanza. Again, to avoid exhaustion of effect he wisely introduces variation. Looking at the following excerpts we can see this refrain in action:

'Into the valley of Death / Rode the six Hundred'

'Into the valley of Death / Rode the six Hundred'

'Into the mouth of hell / Rode the six Hundred'

'Then they rode back, but not / Not the six Hundred'

'All that was left of them / Left of six Hundred'

Noble six hundred!'

While obviously the changes reflect the movement of the Light Brigade into and out of the battle, the inescapable entity is the Light Brigade itself. Note the clever use of caesura and word repetition as they charge back. Look at the dramatic pause after 'Then they rode back', which allows the reader a brief moment of contemplation, which is then coloured with sadness by the repetition of 'not'. Ditto for the repetition of 'left'; it is simple, but devastating. Tennyson concentrates on the collective, the six hundred, rather than any individual, which would have amplified the potential for sympathy from the reader. At the end of the poem it is impossible to forget the six hundred and not only that but due to his clever variations, what lingers is the last trumpeting line, celebrating the nobility of these fighting men.

Of all the repeated phrases used by Tennyson surely it is the 'Honour...Honour' couplet in the final stanza that is most important. This drives home the expected emotional response for the reader and it is hard to argue with the events as described in the poem. The other significant example is Tennyson's condensation of the soldier's duty on the battlefield: 'Theirs not to make reply / Theirs not to reason why / Theirs but to do and die.' Whilst espousing the bravery of the men themselves for Tennyson's Victorian audience, it also leaves itself open to exploitation in the name of propaganda. Again, the First World War and the senseless losses suffered on both sides springs to a modern mind.

Order vs. chaos

The first thing notable about Tennyson's form is its irregularity: Six stanzas of varying lengths: eight lines, nine lines, nine lines, 12 lines, 11 lines and finally six lines. Such irregularity is unusual in Victorian poetry. The rhyming scheme adds to the tension between regularity and irregularity. It is clearly irregular, as it varies from stanza to stanza, but the reoccurrence of certain units in the stanzas lends familiarity and maybe the illusion of regularity. Visually the individual rhyme schemes look like this:

ABCBDDCB   AABCDDDEC

AAABCCDCB   AAABCDDEDCFC

AAABCCCDCEB   AABAAB.

There is clearly variation in each stanza. Not one has the same rhyme scheme but the occurrence of couplets and triplets is common. A strong connection between all the stanzas is Tennyson's imperfect rhyme with the word 'hundred'. He uses 'blundered', 'thundered' and 'wondered' towards the beginning of each stanza with the 'hundred' always the last word in the stanza. Obviously, Tennyson repeatedly brings the attention of the reader to the 'six hundred', but the three rhyme words can be seen to encapsulate the entire poem: the miscommunication, the peril, the glory.

Constant pulling between regularity and irregularity creates a somewhat destabilized feel which mirrors the descent into chaos that confronts the Light Brigade. It also could link to the chaos of war trying to be controlled by military organization. The emphasis on planning and strategy in military operations is key but can be undone simply by the pure haphazard nature of conflict itself.

Of course, Tennyson's use of metre is crucial. He chooses a rare form: the amphimaceric tetrameter. While sounding like a small yet vital gauge in an airplane cockpit, it simply means that Tennyson predominantly uses three syllable combinations that sound like tum-ti-tum. Of course, there's no need for you to use such technical language for GCSE. The crucial thing is to notice that the metre mimics the sound of the thundering, charging horses.

The structure of the poem is almost narrative driven. Again, the structure is not symmetrical but yet there is a clear reflection, albeit a distorted one. We see the charge into enemy lines mirrored by the retreat back, but there is also the treatment of the fatal blunder in stanza two, which technically should start the poem. Tennyson instead chooses to start the poem in media res, as

143

they are charging. This creates a real sense of excitement at the start instead, which may not have been achievable if sticking to a strictly chronological structure. He does get the end of the poem spot on as it builds to a suitably celebratory climax.

Balaclava

The historical Charge of the Light Brigade was a charge of British cavalry led by Lord Cardigan against Russian forces during the Battle of Balaclava on 25  October 1854 in the Crimean War. Lord Raglan, overall commander, intended to send the Light Brigade to pursue and harry a retreating Russian artillery battery near the front line, a task well suited to light cavalry. Due to miscommunication at some level in the chain of command, the sabre-armed Light Brigade was instead sent on a frontal assault into a different artillery battery, one well-prepared with excellent fields of defensive fire. Although reaching the battery under withering direct fire and scattering some of the gunners, the badly mauled brigade was forced to retreat immediately, producing no decisive gains and very high British casualties. Blame for the miscommunication has remained controversial, as the original order from Raglan itself was vague. Tennyson read about it in The Times and wrote the poem minutes later.

LORD RAGLAN

The Charge crunched:

LEAGUE – ONWARD – DEATH – RODE – FORWARD – VALLEY – SIX HUNDRED – LIGHT BRIGADE – DISMAYED – SOLDIER – BLUNDERED – THEIRS – REASON – DIE – VALLEY – SIX HUNDRED – CANNON – LEFT – FRONT – THUNDERED – STORMED – BOLDLY – JAWS – MOUTH – SIX HUNDRED – SABRES – FLASHED – GUNNERS – ARMY – WONDERED – PLUNGED – BROKE – COSSACK – REELED – SHATTERED – CANNON – LEFT – BEHIND – VOLLEYED – SHELL – HERO – FOUGHT – DEATH – HELL – LEFT OF THEM - SIX HUNDRED – GLORY – WILD – WONDERED – HONOUR – LIGHT BRIGADE – NOBLE

Thomas Hardy, *The Man He Killed*

Less can be more

'Grandiloquence' is a word sometimes associated with Victorian literature and Victorian poetry in particular. It means language that is extravagant, designed to impress, language that is rather puffed up and even pompous. A grandiloquent poem is one in which the diction and phrasing have been inflated as if by over-vigorous working of a bicycle pump, and varnished by over-vigorous application of elbow grease. Propagandist poetry aiming to inspire men to join up for WWI also tended towards the grandiloquent. Take, for example, these lines from an early Isaac Rosenberg poem exhorting men to war: 'Flash, mailed seraphim / your burning spears /New days to outflame their dim /Heroic years...' and compare this heightened idiom to his later, grittier, more grounded war poems, such as *Dead Man's Dump*.

One of the most remarkable aspects of Hardy's poem *The Man He Killed* [1902] is the complete absence of verbal padding or straining for magniloquence. In fact, lean, clean and stark, Hardy's style in this dramatic monologue, written in the voice of an ordinary soldier, is the polar opposite. Language doesn't get much plainer, starker or more direct than lines such as 'Had he and I but met, or 'I shot at him as he at me'. Each word is a simple, common monosyllable and these are arranged in the simplest of syntax too. In the first example, that small word 'but' is made to carry tremendous weight and significance. But for one twist of fate the two anonymous men might easily have been friends. With its balanced, mirroring structure the syntax in the second example powerfully conveys the idea that the men are two sides of the same coin. A poet once defined poetry as using the fewest words for the most powerful impact. By this standard, Hardy's simple, spare style manages to be as least as expressive as more grandiloquent poetry.

Clear enough

The narrator presents his account in straightforward, rather stark terms. Simplicity in vocabulary is matched by a swift metre that leaves little time to pause, consider or reflect. Each brief quatrain runs along three short lines of

 trimeter with a slightly longer penultimate line of tetrameter and a simple cross rhyme scheme. Mostly the tone is business-like and matter-of-fact, sticking to the facts of what happened, 'and [I] killed him in his place'. In the third stanza the narrator seems, however, to become more troubled. He feels the need to explain again why he had to kill this man. A hyphen at the end of the first line combined with the repetition of the explanatory word, 'because' create a pause, suggesting a moment of

uncertainty. This uncertainty continues with the abrupt and unexpected internal rhyme of 'so', followed by another pause, a caesura, and the reiteration of the fact that the man was a 'foe' creating another awkwardly jarring internal rhyme. Repetition of this word 'foe' makes it sound rather archaic in this context, like some sort of outdated concept. The inverted syntax adds to the hesitant, stop-start movement of this stanza, 'Just so: my foe of course he was'. Another off-hand sounding phrase 'that's clear enough', like 'just so' and 'of course', rings ironically and hollowly. And immediately after this phrase, the speaker seems to have further doubts about his own assertions, 'although...'.

Whereas the two previous and the two following stanzas end neatly with full stops, enjambment connects the unfinished thought in the last line in this middle stanza to the opening of the following one. Working against the overt sentiments and apparent confidence of the words, the four hyphens in this fourth stanza are a continuing indication of internal conflict, underlying uncertainty and hesitation. Again, the speaker links himself to the dead enemy, assuming that his 'foe' may have joined the army 'off-hand like' just as the speaker had done. Sympathetically, he assumes too that the dead man also shared a need for employment, being 'out of work'. It's a typically frank acknowledgement that the speaker did not join the army out of any romantic, heroic or patriotic notions. He just needed the work, simple as that; there was 'no other reason why'.

A troubled conscience

The final stanza begins with two euphemistic adjectives. Calling war and the twist of fate that led this speaker to kill that man he had no personal animosity for 'quaint and curious' is horribly, bitterly inadequate. This could, perhaps, indicate the speaker's inability to really comprehend his brutal experience. Pushing this further we could suggest this language implies a kind of brutish insensitivity. But, I think, Hardy's point is more that this unnamed, everyman narrator doesn't have the language to express his complex and ambivalent feelings. His conflict is internal and unresolved: Relief at his own survival is mixed with pity for his victim. And more than pity a sense of genuine empathy. It would be easier on the speaker's conscience if he gave in to the temptation of thinking his victim to be some sort of monster, or himself as some sort of hero following a noble cause. The switch in the last stanza from labelling his victim as a clearly demarcated 'foe' to simply a 'fellow', a friendly, familial word, underlines the speaker's ambivalence.

Thomas Hardy was, of course, a novelist as well as a poet. Among his most famous novels are *Tess of the D'Urbervilles*, *Far from the Madding Crowd* and *Jude the Obscure*. In *The Man He Killed*, Hardy's novelistic skills come to the fore. He creates a distinct character and a strong sense of voice. And this soldier is also clearly an ordinary, decent man with generous instincts. Ordinarily he'd share a drink with this other man, 'treat' him and even give him money if he needed it. He has done his duty in war, but remains troubled and conflicted by his killing of another ordinary human being, and he has some sense that the ordinary soldiers might have more in common with each other than they have with other people, such as their own commanding officers perhaps. The outer form of the poem expresses the character's outward appearance - business-like, unsentimental, neat, regular, brusque even. But the novelist ensures that closer up, behind the orderly facade, we are able to detect the signs of a strained and conflicted conscience.

The Man He Killed crunched:

BUT - INN - WE - NIPPERKIN - INFANTRY - FACE - SHOT - KILLED - DEAD - BECAUSE - FOE - ALTHOUGH - PERHAPS - JUST - WORK - REASON - QUAINT - FELLOW - TREAT - HELP

Wilfred Owen, *Anthem for Doomed Youth*

What would you say was the single most remarkable thing about Owen's WWI poem? His skilful use of sonic devices to create the sound scape of battle, such as the 'the stuttering rifle's rapid rattle/ can patter out', which mimics the rat-a-tat-tat of machine gun fire? Or the conceit of the absence of funeral rites for these dead soldiers? Or, perhaps, that immediately striking, brutal first simile that tells us the men are being slaughtered; for 'these who die as cattle'. Alternatively, you might suggest Owen's use of the sonnet form for a poem about war, but also about love. All of these are remarkable features, but, in my opinion the most remarkable thing about the poem is something absent from it, partisanship or animosity towards the enemy, the Germans.

The Hun

To fully appreciate how remarkable this absence is we have to wind the clock back and think ourselves into a young man's mind. An average young man, inspired to take up arms to defend his country, defend Europe, in fact, from German aggression. A young man who had swallowed all the propaganda he had been fed about the Great War, how it was going to a terrific, once-in-a-lifetime adventure, how he was going to return a hero, how the war was going to be short and swift, how the enemy was some sort of ravening, brutish monster that had to be stopped. In particular the mother country and her women needed protecting from the German beast. Here's 'The Hun', depicted in American propaganda as a sort of giant King Kong type ape-monster  making off with a semi-naked, helpless damsel. This image may be American, but British ones were just as bad. Demonizing your enemy, of course, is a common strategy in propaganda. Probably by the time the Great War had begun the average English Tommy had been brainwashed into thinking of the Germans soldiers as brutal, brainless monsters.

Inevitable corollaries to anti-German feeling at a time of war were nationalistic and jingoistic fervour about England and Englishness. Read, for example, Rupert Brooke's *The Soldier*, a celebratory hymn to England, to catch the flavour of these sentiments. Of course, as the title indicates patriotism is expressed in *Anthem for Doomed Youth*, except that the national boundaries of England and Germany have been replaced by a generational one, the 'doomed youth' of both nations. Owen's poem is as much a lament for young, dead German soldiers as it is for the young English dead. At a time of war, considering the context of virulent propaganda, this seems a remarkable triumph of empathy.

It's an odd sort of anthem. Think of national anthems for a moment. Imagine you are a committee choosing a new one for a new country. What are you looking for? What are the key attributes of a successful national anthem? That it should be uplifting, stir the soul, have a feeling of grandeur and an impressive scale. That it should celebrate the unique identity of the country and its history. Think of Land of Hope and Glory. Last night of the proms. Owen's poem certainly isn't rousing. It's a dirge or a lament, a song for the dead. Owen's choice of the word 'anthem' is, then, bitterly ironic.

What passing-bells

As we mentioned at the start of this essay, Owen's poem is constructed around an extended metaphor, technically known as a conceit, comparing the soldiers' deaths on the battlefield with the rituals of a funeral: Rather than having 'passing-bells' the men are led away to be brutally and casually slaughtered, like 'cattle'; instead of last prayers [orisons] for their eternal souls, they have the pounding of artillery and the rattle of rifle fire; instead of mourners and a choir they have wailing shells and bugles. In the second stanza, the sonnet's sestet, instead of candles, the only 'holy glimmers' they will see are in each other's eyes before death comes; rather than a funeral pall over their coffin they will have only the pale faces of their loved ones left behind in England and in lieu of flowers they will have only these women's tenderness. Finally, instead of having the blinds drawn as a sign of mourning, these men will face a greater darkness, that of eternal night falling. The implication is that not only are these men being led to slaughter, but that their sacrifice is not even adequately acknowledged or mourned for, let alone honoured. Perhaps even their chance of an afterlife is being denied. By whom? By the army, perhaps, and also by a population back home who had little idea of the true horrors - the gas attacks, going over the top, the barbed wire, the dead and dying in no-man's-land, the rats, the lice, the endless mud, the dead bodies, the ceaseless pounding of the big guns, the closeness of death, the blasted landscapes - of prolonged trench warfare. Like his friend and fellow war poet, Siegfried Sassoon, Owen wanted to puncture the complacency of the civilian population and try to get over to them the realities, truth and pity of the Great War.

So, perhaps, rather than the Germans, the real enemies were the callousness of the Generals sending men to be butchered and the indifference of the civilian population and the politicians who continued the war. Certainly Sassoon thought so and he famously said so in a letter published in The Times newspaper. Sassoon would have faced the severest of military discipline if his friends had not managed to plead he was suffering from temporary insanity and ship him off to Craiglockhart hospital in Scotland where he would meet Owen for the first time. But there's another enemy in this poem and it appears in many of Owen's WWI poems.

Machine war

Sometimes in Owen's poems it can appear that nature and perhaps even God have either abandoned or worse actively turned against the soldiers. But a more persistent threat is the technology of warfare. WWI was the first 'machine war'. Though machine guns had been used previously, in the Boer

War for instance, the ones used in WWI were far more efficient and far more deadly. Added to this was the new horror of gas shells and towards the end of the war, tanks and fighter planes. In *Anthem for Doomed Youth* Owen uses personification in a bitterly ironic way. It seems that as the men are dying helplessly the machines are taking on a life and a will of their own. It is almost as if the weaponry is acting of its own accord, following its own mad logic without any human influence. There is a monster here, but it's not the

German army; Owen describes the sound of the big guns [English and German] as 'monstrous anger'. He also uses the adjective 'stuttering' to describe rifle fire. This word suggests the intermittentness of the firing, but also implies that the rifles might jam. More importantly, it is as if the weapons are speaking - they 'patter out' the men's prayers. 'Patter out', of course, can mean 'make the sound of', but also implies cancelling out, erasing. The shells are also personified, as a choir of 'shrill, demented' voices, 'wailing'. The madness and anger and monstrosity of the war seems to emanate from the technology and the soldiers are helpless before it.

Noticeably the imagery in the first stanza is predominantly aural. We hear the discordant din of battle, the anger, the stuttering, the wailing, guns, rifles, shells, bugles. The imagery of the second stanza is more visual and the tone more elegiac. In particular, Owen uses the symbolism of light, specifically light going out in references to candles, eyes, glimmers, pallor and finally dusk falling.

Owen's poem has to stand in for the absent mourning and funeral rites for the dead soldiers. He offers his own lament as a way of honouring these inescapably 'doomed youth'. They were doomed because they faced impossible, insurmountable odds. Yet Owen when he was invalided to Craiglockhart with shellshock and could have sat out the rest of the war, chose to go back and fight alongside his men. Owen had the choice to sit out the rest of the war, but, knowing the full horror of the experience he chose to go back. Why? Because he was a captain in the British army and he could not bear the thought of abandoning his men. It was a decision, of course, that cost him his life at the tender age of just 25. Not only in his poetry then, but with his life, Owen  demonstrated his deep respect, compassion and sense of honour for his fellow soldiers, German as well as English.

Anthem for Doomed Youth crunched:

CATTLE - MONSTROUS - RATTLE - PATTER - PRAYERS - CHOIRS - DEMENTED - BUGLES - SPEED - EYES - GOOD-BYES - PALL - TENDERNESS - DUSK

Keith Douglas, *Vergissmeinnicht*

The tanks that broke the ranks

They say that the First World War was the first modern war. Certainly, it was the beginning of the end for traditional hand-to-hand combat, as rifles and bayonets and horses, the symbols of centuries of warfare, began to be replaced by long-range artillery, bomber planes, trenches, chemical attacks and tanks. But it was during the Second World War that the lethal potential and terrifying implications of the new species of impersonal and deathless mechanical weapons began to be fully recognised and exploited. This new ability to kill [or to be killed] remotely, without having to look the enemy in the eye and sense a shared humanity, meant that killing became yet more dispassionate, breeding a cynicism which built on the already-tarnished reputation of the 'glorious war'. The poets of the Second World War responded by producing a body of work which detailed their experiences in an impassive, unsentimental voice. And none was more unsentimental than Keith Douglas.

Douglas had completed his officer training at Sandhurst in February 1941 and, after a brief stint with the 2nd Derbyshire Yeomanry, had been transferred to the Sherwood Rangers, and posted first to Palestine and then to Egypt. Egypt was a key territory in the Western Desert campaign, and El Alamein, the site of a railway halt, was one of its most strategically important regions. It was there [as the name suggests] that the Second Battle of El Alamein took place: a brutal conflict with vicious encounters between opposing divisions of armoured vehicles, which cost the Axis around 50,000 men and 500 tanks in the three weeks of fighting, and the Allies some 14,000

and 400 of the same. On the third day of the battle, after disobeying an order to remain behind, Douglas had led his tank division into the fray, and before long had been hit  square by the shell of an anti-tank gun. It was a face-to-face encounter with death, and yet, remarkably, none of his crew was killed, and they managed to destroy the gun-pit before it could fire on them again.

Three weeks passed and the battle finished, and Douglas and his men returned 'over the nightmare ground' and 'found the place' where their tank had been hit. They found, too, the bloated and rotting corpse of the soldier who had attacked them unsuccessfully, and whom they had killed, sprawled in the shadow of his anti-tank gun. It was this experience that provided the narrative for *Vergissmeinnicht*, one of Douglas' most celebrated poems, and one in which he most powerfully evoked the desensitising effect of the new mechanical warfare.

Cleanin' my rifle [and dreamin' of you]

A key conceit for Douglas in capturing this cynicism and callousness is his blurring of the boundary between animate and inanimate, between flesh and blood and cold hard steel. As the soldiers are losing their humanity, Douglas seems to suggest, their weapons are gaining it. In the second stanza, for example, he personifies the 'frowning' barrel of the dead man's gun, ascribing it a human face with the vaguely displeased expression of the cartoon Army General: an expression whose indifference fails to convey the full horror of the blood-soaked scene. Later, Douglas has the adjective 'gunpit' qualify the unusual noun 'spoil', which can mean valuable items which have been pillaged or stolen, or the arms and armour of a slain enemy, but can also mean the uneaten remains of an animal carcass. Part of the effect here is in demonstrating that the poet has grown insensitive to death and suffering, and feels little guilt in dehumanising the dead German, reducing him to meat for scavengers to pick at. But part of the effect, again, is in  breathing life into the inanimate steel: 'spoil' can be read as referring to the remnants of the destroyed 'gunpit', with the poet reimagining the ruined weapon as a dead and mutilated body, the machinery once more ascribed the attributes of a living creature.

159

Douglas extends this conceit when he describes how the dead soldier's lethal 'equipment' is 'mocking' the man who once operated it, attributing to the weapon the capability of human-to-human interaction. And when those two lines are read in full – 'mocked at by his own equipment / that's hard and good when he's decayed' – a sexual euphemism playing on 'equipment' and 'hard' becomes unmistakable. The lines provide more evidence of the cold-heartedness which the war has engendered in the speaker, in this case by recording the crude-ish joke he's made about a guy he's killed. But the image of the still-living weapon, unhurt and un-decayed, laughing at the frailty of the human body, also projects a vision of a world in which the machines have outlived their operators. Sex is a symbol of life, vitality and the continuation of the species, and is one of the fundamental interactions between humans. The dead soldier's 'decayed equipment' – his sexual impotency – therefore, reflects the broader demise of common human interaction, the loss of sympathy and sensitivity, and reads as a forecast of extinction.

There is a definite sense that the inanimate weapons have taken control of the soldiers' actions; that the soldiers have become more a tool of the weapons than vice versa. After all, 'mockery' isn't a balanced human interaction: it establishes a hierarchy which, in this instance, places the dead man's 'own equipment' above him. This reversed-ranking was hinted at in the poem's second stanza, where Douglas describes the barrel of the German's gun 'overshadowing' him – 'overshadow' can of course mean 'to cast a shadow over', but its other meaning of 'to diminish the relative importance of' is equally relevant here. And the peculiar simile, 'like the entry of a demon', in that same stanza introduces a motif of demonic enchantment, as if the rise of mechanical weaponry has acted like an malicious spirit, possessing the soldiers and driving them to cruelty. It's a motif which seems to be continued in the poem's final stanza where, in the line 'And Death who had the soldier singled', Douglas appears to portray himself as the Grim Reaper [he killed the man, after all]. No wonder, then, that those still living feel distant and callous: they've lost their compassion, and they've surrendered control to the pitiless demon of war.

Don't let's be beastly to the Germans

In another of his poems, Desert Flowers, Douglas acknowledged his debt to the First World War poet, Isaac Rosenberg: 'Rosenberg I only repeat what you were saying'. But the narrative of Vergissmeinnicht is more reminiscent of a work by another Great War poet, Wilfred Owens, titled Strange Meeting. In that poem a soldier enters the underworld and meets an enemy soldier he had killed the previous day, just as Douglas returned and saw the man his crew had killed. Douglas' poem, though, is far more cynical and far less conciliatory than Owens', with the mutual respect and pity which the soldiers of Strange Meeting exhibit replaced by cruelty and derision and little success in taking a non-partisan view of the slaughter.

The gloating tone of the 'equipment' pun is far from the only instance of the speaker's mercilessness. He plays on the idiom 'with contempt' in the line 'We see him almost with content', simultaneously conveying the disdain the men feel towards the German and their delight in seeing him dead. He contrasts their nonchalant response with that of the dead man's lover who 'would weep', reinforcing the lack of tears with the image of the dry 'dust' on the 'paper eye', and seeming to revel in his breezy description of the swarming flies and the erupted belly. And he casts scorn on the signed photograph which they find among the soldier's possessions, a gift from his girlfriend back home, with the bathos of 'who has put' initiating the sneering tone, and the childish connotations of 'copybook' writing reinforcing it.

The adjective 'gothic' seems pointedly chosen, too: though it is commonly used to refer to the blackletter typeface often associated with written German, the word can also mean 'barbaric' or 'savage' or, most pertinently, 'in bad taste'. These alternative connotations serve to convey the speaker's feeling that the woman's gift too soppy and sentimental, and the Hollywood overtones of the carefully-placed 'script', coupled with the fact that *Vergissmeinnicht*, as well as being an expression and the name of a flower, was the title of a saccharine German love song from that era, certainly suggests that he thinks little of the sugar-coated romanticism on display.

 Moreover, the speaker seems determined to destroy any vestige of genuine emotion which the signed photograph may carry, insisting that it has been 'dishonoured' – there's a chance he means that it has been sullied by its proximity to death, but it seems more likely, considering the gloating tone elsewhere, that he means the girl has been dishonoured because her boyfriend lost the battle and got himself killed.

There is almost no honour paid to the dead throughout the poem, culminating in the final stanza which, despite its celebrated delineation of the soldier's twin identities, 'the lover and killer', reads more like a parody of wartime oration than a heart-felt reflection on the complex cruelty of war. The self-consciously Latinate inversion of 'who had the soldier singled', placing the verb at the end, does some of the work; the knowing archaism of 'mortal hurt', borrowed perhaps from Romeo and Juliet, finishes the job. Indeed, there seems to be an attempt to deny the dead German any value at all: that curious pun, 'We see him almost with content', could also be read as 'We see him almost with meaning' or 'with substance', with the implication being, 'Almost, but not quite'. This is supported by a proliferation of words relating to things not being fully real or of full value: 'almost' and 'seeming' are self-explanatory; 'abased' can mean 'degraded' / 'humbled', and can be used as a synonym for when currency is debased; 'mocked' contains the root 'mock' which can mean 'imitation' or 'counterfeit'. The dead German is unreal, the girlfriend's suffering is unreal – it's hard to find meaning and value, it seems, in the middle of the War.

Down forget-me-not lane

And yet, in that line, 'We see him almost with content', there is the feeling that Douglas and his crew are trying to see the dead German as real and valuable, but are simply unable to do so. The foregrounded opposition between that line and 'But she would weep to see today' demonstrates that the speaker recognises that the  matter is purely subjective, that his perception of the situation is bound to be biased. He is, perhaps, more enlightened than others in acknowledging that, really, the German's life was worth no less than his own, at least to some people. But he is not so advanced as to be able to shed his patriotism and ingrained hatred of the Hun. History is written by the winning side, as it is here, and the sense of history – or, more, the sense of regression – runs strongly through the poem.

There are the archaisms highlighted above, to which might be added 'combatants', 'dishonoured' [with its connotations of chivalry], 'gothic' [in the sense of 'Germanic'], 'spoil' and 'swart'. They are words of earlier confrontations, with the Goths, with the 'swarthy' fighters of the Ottoman Empire, in which honour could be won and lost, and the spoils of war were the ready reward. And now they have resurfaced, lost once but returned again, as the repetition of 'gone' and 'found' in the poem's first stanza implies. The weapons may be different, but the inability to avoid bloodshed which marks millennia human existence is just as powerful as ever. Douglas sees in the scene, and in his own reaction to the sight of the dead German, a powerful hand dragging him back into the past, into the primitive 'cave' of the man's 'burst stomach', which recalls not only rudimentary human life, but Plato's allegory of enlightenment [and the lack of it]. The 'dust' on the dead man's eye isn't just the sand of the desert: it's a reminder of the repetition of history and the inevitability of death; the same dust as in T.S. Eliot's 'I will show you fear in a handful of dust'; the same dust as the Bible's 'you are dust, and to dust you shall return'.

Douglas is suffering from a painful contradiction: there are faint traces of sympathy for the dead man, most evident in 'nightmare', perhaps, or 'who had one body and one heart'; but he is unable to escape the machinations of the civilisation which would have him feel no pity for the enemy, and has found his powers of compassion blunted by the remoteness and lottery of mechanised warfare. The inconsistency of the rhyme scheme – which shifts between ABBA, ABAB and AABB – and the use of pararhymes, which clashes, for example, 'heart' and 'hurt', seem to be a poetic embodiment of this contradiction. The gesture towards a rhyme-pattern is an attempt to make coherence and lyricism from brutality; the 'failure' of the rhyme scheme is the triumph of savagery and cynicism.

Vergissmeinnicht crunched:

COMBATANTS – NIGHTMARE – AGAIN – SPRAWLING – FROWNING – OVERSHADOWING – TANK – DEMON – SPOIL – DISHONOURED – VERGISSMEINNICHT – COPYBOOK – GOTHIC – CONTENT – ABASED – MOCKED – HARD – WEEP – SWART – DUST – CAVE – MINGLED – BODY – DEATH – MORTAL

Ted Hughes, *Bayonet Charge*

Inspired by the great war poets. such as Wilfred Owen, and by the stories of his father's exploits in World War One, Hughes' poem examines the experience of an individual soldier on the battlefield. Moving away from the idea of collective identity and soldiery seen in poems such as *The Charge of the Light Brigade*, Hughes explores the thoughts and feelings of a single soldier as he struggles towards enemy lines. The enemy is not known; neither is the allegiance of the soldier himself, though we might assume he is British due to the possible mention of George V in 'King'. It is the individual soldier's experience that is the focus of this poem - a universal experience. We see the fighting through the febrile eyes of an anonymous soldier, the focus on conflict [both external and internal] rather than country.

Suddenly he awoke

Beginning in media res, *Bayonet Charge* opens with no explanation of what is happening. Like the soldier, we are thrown into a state of confusion. No immediate reason is given as to why the soldier is 'running' – indeed, we are not even explicitly told that the 'he' mentioned is a soldier. Although we are given small details throughout the poem, we are never allowed to know the setting or context as a whole; we remain as disorientated as the soldier is throughout.

The nightmarish opening of 'Suddenly he awoke and was running' bears witness to a soldier 'suddenly' realising the reality and urgency of his situation, the dramatic adverb highlighting his panic. Awaking from the patriotic dream of 'King, honour, human dignity', the soldier is utterly unprepared for the realities of warfare; he runs 'raw - /In raw-seamed hot khaki'. Repetition here emphasises his discomfort – discomfort with his ill-fitting uniform, but also with his role in the conflict. Recalling the phrase 'raw recruits', 'raw' also highlights inexperience and youth, and recalls images of raw meat and cows sent to slaughter. This soldier is not charging boldly towards death; he is terrified, alone, bewildered.

The first stanza showcases the brutal intrusion of reality as the nameless soldier realises the danger he is in. He is overwhelmed by exhaustion and terror. The physical and emotional strain is made clear as he wears his 'hot khaki, his sweat heavy'. The headlong rush of that eleven-line long, breathless first sentence, with its repetitive vocabulary, density of present participle verbs and loose construction, evokes heavy breathing as the soldiers runs and we are never fully certain whether he is panting from exertion or terror. The repeated references to 'sweat' pose a similar dilemma – is the soldier sweating because he is physically drained, or because he is consumed by his terror? Regardless, he is clearly losing control of both the situation and his body. Verbs such as 'stumbling' suggest lack of control over his actions; indeed, the entire line 'stumbling across a field of clods towards a green hedge' creates a choppy, uncertain rhythm, reflecting the soldier's

167

struggle navigating the landscape. He is physically exhausted: his gun is not carried, but 'lugged'. He is disorientated, so 'dazzled' by the rifle fire of enemy lines that he fixes on an inanimate object rather than a specific enemy. His gun is 'numb as a smashed arm', perhaps reflecting his own body shutting down. He, like the gun, feels broken and useless.

Clearly the gun foreshadows the injuries the soldier may suffer and it supports the violent imagery already present in the plosive 'bullets smacking the belly out of the air'. Yet it also symbolises how the soldier has become numb to the reasons why he signed up to fight in the war in the first place. It is interesting that the simile is linked by a semi-colon to the description of 'the patriotic tear that had brimmed in his eye /Sweating like molten iron from the centre of his chest'. The soldier's gun is useless because he is no longer sure what he is fighting for. Patriotism has been shoved aside by a painful reality. It is this, more than the battle itself, which disorientates the

 soldier. Without his patriotic ideals, the world seems to have turned inside out. A 'smashed arm' is a brutal image that we associate with agony, not numbness; the image of 'bullets smacking the belly out of the air' is similarly inverted. Rather than an image of air being punched out of someone, as we expect

when someone is winded, here the 'belly' is being punched out of the air itself. Everything that made sense to the soldier has become lost in the haze of battle. He is like a lost, confused child, echoed in the oddly childlike punishment of 'smacking'.

As the poem progresses, we see the soldier lose progressively more of his individuality until he transforms from a thinking human being into a dangerous weapon. Consumed by fear, he becomes little more than an animal. Like the hare that crawls, 'its mouth wide / Open silent, its eyes standing out', he is unable to express agony and terror. He is voiceless, unable to change his fate – he is, just like the hare, prey. The bathos of 'King, honour, human dignity,' and the tellingly dismissive 'etcetera' clearly shows how futile this ideology is in war; the anticlimactic ending suggesting that the reasons for going to war are no longer even worth mentioning. The soldier attacks out of a desperate desire to survive, not moral principle. In reality, these ideas are mere 'luxuries'; the soldier is reduced to a state of animalistic fear, only able to express himself through a meaningless, unreasoned 'yelling alarm'. By the end of the poem, his nerves are stretched to their limit and he is lost to his explosive fear. We are left with the final metaphor of 'his terror's touchy dynamite', an alliterative image that suggests he is ready to explode at the slightest touch. War has destroyed his patriotic ideals; all that is left is destruction and fear.

He almost stopped

Notably, *Bayonet Charge* does not follow a rhyme scheme or any sort of formal structure. The experience of the soldier is expressed instead through sentence construction, line length, enjambment and pacing. The first stanza showcases the strain the soldier is under, long vowels stretching words and slowing the pace at times to mimic his unsteady progression across the field. The third stanza passes by in a blur of hurtling terror as the soldier loses the capacity for higher reasoning. Yet it is the second, with its long, drawn out contemplation, that is the most interesting.

Contrasting heavily with the first and third stanzas, the poem's middle section is dedicated not to the external, physical conflict the soldier is engaged in, but to the internal one inside his head. A stolen moment of introspection on the battlefield, an entire stanza occurs within the time given it takes to make a single step. Here, we do not see the increasing panic and confusion of the other stanzas; instead, we witness a rational, intelligent man wondering how he got to this terrifying point in his life.

The 'patriotic tear that had brimmed in his eye' gone forever. The soldier is lost in 'bewilderment'. His unthinking obedience to the army falters as, mid-charge, he starts to wonder why he is there. The dash at the end of 'he almost stopped' abruptly shortens the line, pausing the action and creating a sudden stillness that takes the reader out of the conflict and into the soldier's head. Although the stanza still primarily focuses on fear, lingering on the image of 'a man who has jumped up in the dark' and fled from his nightmares, there is a sense of distance here, of emotional detachment. Whilst the quick pace created through enjambment and the repetition of 'running' hurries the stanza along, we do not feel any of the panic or confusion of the previous stanza. Indeed, the juxtaposition between the running man and the calmness of the soldier is only emphasised by the simile 'his foot hung like /Statuary in mid stride'; the sense of immobility reinforced through the following caesura. Sandwiched between the two images of frozen movement, the running man becomes something more than a simplistic idea of fear – he becomes a symbol of the futility of the war.

Running 'in the dark' and listening 'for the reason / Of his still running', the man in this stanza is presented as being both blind and irrational. Unable to see where he is going, or why he is even running, he represents the soldier's sudden realisation of the pointlessness of war. The soldier no longer feels he is fighting for any good reason – he is isolated, alone, part of the bigger picture, but unable to relate to it. When he asks himself 'in what cold clockwork of the stars and the nations /Was he the hand pointing that second?', the soldier has suddenly, fully realised his insignificance. Whilst he is the 'hand' of conflict, a synecdoche for the nation he represents, he is still the 'second' hand; a small, near-meaningless measurement of time. In comparison to the larger units of 'nations' and space, he is irrelevant, miniscule. Like the ticking of the clock, war is inevitable – it does not matter if he is there or not. It will continue regardless. The harsh 'c' and 'k' consonance of 'cold clockwork' emphasises his isolation. He is, he realises, unimportant and his own nation does not care about him.

The green hedge

Between the vivid, onomatopoeic depiction of physical conflict in stanzas one and three, and the internal conflict portrayed in stanza two, it is perhaps easy to forget the third, hidden conflict within Hughes' poem. With the lack of a clearly identifiable enemy, at times it almost feels like the soldier and his allies are attacking Nature itself.

There is a clear message within this poem about the destructive nature of conflict. In the first stanza, the 'field of clods' the soldier runs over are juxtaposed with the 'green hedge' he runs towards. What was once a fertile field, capable of bearing crops has, due to human conflict, become nothing more than lumps of earth. As the soldier charges towards the unspoilt 'green hedge', blending the inanimate object with the enemy firing upon him in his confused state, there is a sense that Nature is under attack by humanity. The image that is strengthened in the final stanza, as the soldier 'plunged past with his bayonet toward the green hedge'. With no mention of an enemy force, it is the repeated imagery of the 'green hedge' that seems to become the soldier's adversary.

The 'shot-slashed furrows' that throw the soldier out of his introspection further reinforces the theme of Man versus Nature; alliterative and hard to say out loud without slowing the pace, it draws our attention to the contrast between growth and destruction. Whilst a farmer would plough the earth to grow crops and create life, here the earth has been changed through the armies' attempts to kill their enemies. Nature, it appears, is sick and dying. The hare is 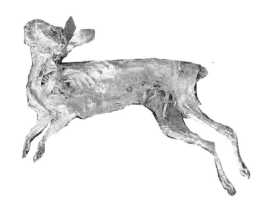 described as 'yellow' – whilst this could symbolise the soldier's own fear due to the typical association of the colour with cowardice. But it also has connotations of sickness and life withering away. Rolling 'like a flame', the hare is in agony. The use of the agricultural term 'threshing' adds to the idea that Nature is devastated by war as the hare writhes in pain. Its helpless, crawling movements reflect the damage mankind is wreaking upon Nature; its terrified expression with 'its mouth wide /Open silent, its eyes standing out' show how vulnerable the hare is.

Human dignity, etcetera

Whilst we can assume that the poem centres on a soldier charging an enemy trench in World War One, Hughes' poem does not hinge on any particular single moment in time. His exploration of both the internal and external conflicts of war, alongside the examination of the effect war has on Nature, allows Hughes to explore the nature of conflict itself. The soldier's experience is a universal one, not tied to any specific battle, or even any particular country. Conflict, Hughes suggests, is both physically and mentally devastating, destroying our natural surroundings and our own sense of self. It is a cold, almost mechanical experience, as inevitable as the progression of time itself. The hare's 'threshing circle' is perhaps not just an expression of agony; it is also a commentary on the nature of conflict itself. Like a circle, it has no end and is pointless. Nothing is really gained. And so much is lost.

Bayonet Charge crunched:

SUDDENLY – AWOKE – RAW – SWEAT – HEAVY – STUMBLING – CLODS – GREEN – HEDGE – SMACKING – NUMB – SMASHED – PATRIOTIC – BEWILDERMENT – STOPPED – COLD – RUNNING – DARK – STATUARY – FURROWS – YELLOW – HARE – CRAWLED – THRESHING – CIRCLE – SILENT – HONOUR – DIGNITY – ETCETERA – LUXURIES – ALARM – DYNAMITE

Owen Sheers, *Mametz Wood*

Chits of bone

Like the painting above by Christopher Williams, Sheers' moving, poignant poem commemorates a bloody attack by the Welsh Fusiliers on a fortified

German position in Mametz wood, one of the many sub-battles of the infamous Battle of the Somme [1916]. The poem seems perfectly suited for a cloze exercise, as this will draw attention to some of the poet's more striking language choices. If you're a teacher, you could present the poem to a class with the following words blanked out: 'wasted young'; 'chit'; 'china plate'; 'relic'; 'bird's egg'; 'nesting'; 'sentinel'; 'wound'; 'foreign body'; 'skin'; 'broken mosaic'; 'socketed'; 'dropped open'; 'notes'; 'sung' and 'absent tongues'. If you're a student, consider what each of this list of words contributes to the poem.

The first phrase, 'wasted young', recalls Wilfred Owen's references to 'doomed youth' and to the soldiers as 'boys'. They are 'wasted' in two senses, both wasted away, decayed, but also, more feelingly, their deaths were a waste. The phrase keeps in mind the fact that some of the soldiers would have been only teenagers when they fought and died in the trenches of WWI.

The next four words and phrases work together to establish the fragility of  the remains and the tenderness with which the poem handles them. A 'chit' is a small piece of paper; hence the metaphor suggests the bones have become very delicate and thin. A 'chit' is often issued for something owed, which raises the idea of what we might owe these men. It can also mean a small child or baby animal. The 'china plate' metaphor enhances the impression, conjuring a visual image of broken crockery. With its religious connotations, 'relic' may take us in a slightly different direction, but also confirms the poet's attitude of veneration for the dead. The last image in this series is the most powerful. Comparing the skull to a 'bird's egg' is visually haunting and conveys the horrible vulnerability of flesh and blood to violence. The overall effect of the second stanza is enhanced by Sheers' use of sonic devices. In the first line, emphatic metre picks out the important words:

'A chit of bone, the china plate of a shoulder blade'

Alliteration of 'ch' modulates into the softer 'sh' and 'bone' alliterates with 'blade'; assonantal rhyme connects 'plate' to 'blade' and 'china plate' near rhymes with 'shoulder blade'. The 'pl' and 'bl' sounds are echoed in the next line, combining with the full rhyme of '<u>b</u>one', giving '<u>bl</u>own' greater emphasis. These plosive and assonantal sounds climax in '<u>b</u>roken <u>b</u>ird'.

Similarly, Sheers uses imagery and sound for emphasis in the reference to the machine guns in the next stanza. Metaphorically they are 'nesting', an image that recalls the 'bird's egg' and might make us think of cuckoos or other birds which steal other birds' nests. The terrible factual detail that soldiers in the Somme were ordered to 'walk, not run' into gunfire is powerful enough by itself, but in a poem in which end rhyme is used only here, the couplet it forms with 'guns' is especially effective and affecting.

Even now the earth stands sentinel

'Sentinel' obviously makes us think of military guards or look-outs. Personifying the 'earth' in this way creates a counterbalance to the idea that the soldiers' lives were 'wasted'. It is as if nature now guards them because they are precious and her own. Though nothing can be done to help these dead men, the poem suggests that, like 'the earth' what we can do is honour and remember them. Personification continues in the image of the earth as a wounded victim of war working out a 'foreign body'. Like the simple references to time, 'for years', 'even now', it reminds us how long lasting, how deep the devastation of the war was and how widespread; a hundred years on and the land is still recovering, and still uncovering more dead.

The broken dead

Sheers has already presented the men's body as fragments, bits of body parts - bone, skull, shoulder-blades. And these fragments are themselves 'broken'. Found buried together, the bodies are a 'broken mosaic' and the skulls of some are missing jaws. In a horrible irony, their worthless boots have 'outlasted them'. And yet the men seem almost alive - their skeletons have been 'paused mid dance macabre', as if the poet or time could press a button and set them moving again in a morbid dance of life-in-death. The image of their 'socketed' heads is another morbid one, but set against this brokenness and morbidity is the men's emphatic togetherness. They are a 'they'; one 'mosaic'; 'their' heads and 'their skeletons', and, most poignantly, even in death they are 'linked arm in arm'.

The men obviously cannot sing or indeed tell their story. But this 'unearthing' - the revelation of their graves - prompts another unearthing of their story, this poem, the words Sheers has used, the reading of it in every reader's mind. In this way, Sheers, like the earth, stands sentinel over these men's grave and offers his voice to speak for their 'absent tongues'.

Why, you might ask, has Sheers written the poem in tercets - three-lined stanzas? Good question and the truth is, I don't know. There is, however, something delicate about tercets in comparison to more robust quatrains. And Sheers adds to this delicacy through using quite long lines stretched out across the page. Maybe he was thinking too of the three central relationships in the poem - the soldiers, nature and us. Like the poet, we did not experience the horrors these young men suffered. All we can do is to continue to honour and remember their sacrifice, and stand like sentinels to their memories for the sake of future generations.

Mametz Wood crunched:

AFTERWARDS - WASTED - TENDED - BONE - FINGER - SKULL - MIMICKED - WALK - GUNS - SENTINEL - BACK - WOUND - GRAVE - MOSAIC - SKELETONS - OUTLASTED - HEADS - OPEN - SUNG - UNEARTHING - ABSENT

Jane Weir, *Poppies*

Holding on/ letting go

A poem dramatising the parental conflict between wanting to hold on to and protect one's children and the need to let them go and live their own lives, *Poppies* articulates every parent's worst fear - that their child may come to harm. And knowing this might be the case, of course, only makes the letting go even harder to bear.

Weir's poem is full of deliberately unclear time shifts. Time collapses, for instance, as the mother switches between memories of her son leaving to go to school and her son leaving to go to war. The speaker longs to hold on to her son, trying to turn back time so that the poem ends with her 'hoping to hear' her son's 'playground voice catching on the wind'. Time, the poem suggests, is fleeting. The wind, often a metaphor for elusiveness, clearly shows that both youth and memory are transitory and intangible; an idea that is particularly tragic in a poem so heavily dominated by physical textures and

179

the senses. Whilst the alliteration of 'hoping to hear' captures how hard the mother strains to hear her son and recapture their close relationship from his childhood, we know that her attempts are futile.

Right from the start, the mother contrasts her personal loss with the grief of the nation. Repetition of 'before', in 'Three days before Armistice Sunday' and 'Before you left', highlights how precious the time before her son left was to the mother. The 'individual war graves', an ominous reminder of the cost of war, are juxtaposed with the distancing of the son from his mother as he leaves her. Here we see the first of numerous blurrings of time, as we are left to question whether the mother is remembering attaching a poppy to the schoolboy uniform of her child or to the 'blazer' of an adult soldier's dress uniform. The 'yellow bias binding' could signal either the smart finish on a school uniform, or the rank and regiment of a soldier. The metaphor of the 'blockade', however, is a clear, unambiguous sign of how the mother feels shut out of her son's life.

This 'binding' is part of the poem's semantic fields of imprisonment and liberation, key themes that run through the poem. There is a sense that perhaps the mother feels aggrieved by the military's 'binding' of her son to them, that she is secretly pleased to '[disrupt] a blockade' with her pinned poppy and stake her claim. However, we can also interpret this image as the complete opposite – that the pinning of the poppy, a symbol now irrevocably linked with the military, disrupts the 'yellow bias' of a blazer that reminds her of his childhood, representing the military's cutting of the ties between mother and son. It is just one of several ambiguous images within a poem that resists definitive interpretation.

Whilst the 'Sellotape bandaged around my hand' can be read as a metaphor for both the mother's emotional wounds and her son's potential future wounds, it also reflects how the mother's hands are figuratively tied. As much as she would like to keep her son within the domestic sphere and protect him, she cannot prevent him leaving. Nowhere is this clearer than in the third stanza, when separation finally takes places. Here, the 'front door' becomes a symbol of the dangerous outside world, a metaphor for the son's crossing of the boundary between the protected domestic and the unprotected public spheres. Unable to deny herself the opportunity to cling to their last few moments together, the mother congratulates herself for being 'brave, as I walked /with you, to the front door'. Her throwing open of the door is emotional, almost aggressive, emphasised by the sudden shift into rhyme, and forms a last challenge to the world that will take her son away. Her son shows less grief over their parting and is gone in a 'split second'. For him, the world is full of potential, 'overflowing /like a treasure chest', a simile that shows the excitement he feels at the freedom that awaits.

Like the 'song bird' the mother releases from the 'cage' in her son's bedroom, the son is free of the gilded cage of affection his mother has placed him in. It is no coincidence that the very next line describes how 'a

single dove flew from the pear tree': it is a clear metaphor for the son's liberation. Ancient Chinese mythology portrays the pear tree as a symbol of longevity and immortality; Weir appears to be implying that, whilst he has left the security of home for the more dangerous outside world, the son has achieved a measure of independence and freedom as shown by his 'single' status. Whilst the poem may end with the mother's hopeless straining to recapture her son's childhood, it also ends with her son free and unrestrained as the 'dove pulled freely against the sky'.

Inscriptions on the war memorial

As a textile designer, it is perhaps unsurprising that Weir roots much of *Poppies* in textures and physical contact. Much of the connection that the mother has with her son is expressed through tactile imagery, whether this comes from pinning the 'crimped petals' of a paper poppy to her son's lapel, removing cat hairs, or grazing noses in Eskimo kisses. For the mother, touch provides a physical connection that is stronger than memory and allows her to express her affection. Her memory of how she 'smoothed down your shirt's /upturned collar' is onomatopoeic; long double vowel sounds mimic her soothing, domestic motions and how much she cares. The 'gelled /blackthorns' of the son's hair, however, whilst also reminiscent of Christ's crown of thorns, are physical representations of the distance that grows between the mother and her son even before he leaves. Sharp and unwelcoming, the 'blackthorns' are a metaphor for how now the son has grown up; the mother is no longer able to freely touch him. With a relationship so heavily reliant on physical affection, it is perhaps to be expected that after the mother's touch is denied she complains that 'All my words /flattened, rolled, turned into felt'. With touch removed, the mother finds herself unable to fully articulate her emotions and communicate with her son, her voice crushed in a similar way to that of the felt used to make military caps.

The semantic field of textiles and sewing within the poem gives the mother a defined, domestic voice, emphasising her nurturing side through the allusions to the taking care of her son's clothes [and her son] over the years. The poem's early focus on the maintenance of her son's clothing – such as his 'blazer' and the 'upturned collar' of his shirt – provides a telling contrast to the later image of the mother being 'hat-less, without /a winter coat or reinforcements of scarf, gloves'. If clothing imagery reflects her bond with her son, it appears that without him the mother is left vulnerable and exposed. The military reference of 'reinforcements' only heightens this vulnerability, whilst also presenting us with the juxtaposition of the two worlds her son now belongs to. The mother seems increasingly consumed by anxiety over her son's fate: the image of her 'stomach busy /making tucks, darts, pleats' uses symbols of the domestic sphere to vividly depict her fears; the simple idea of a stomach knotted with anxiety transforms into striking imagery that almost tips into the realm of magical realism. Full of hard consonants and one-syllable words, the triple list mimics the sharp stabs of pain that accompany the mother's fear.

The continued use of sewing imagery only strengthens our understanding of the mother's fear in the final stanza, as she seeks to replace her lost physical bond with her son through the touching of objects she associates with him. The tracing of 'the inscriptions on the war memorial' allows her to form a tangible connection with her son, yet also hints at her fear that he too will someday end up carved upon it. The memorial's solidity contrasts distinctly with the imagery of the 'ornamental stitch' of the dove in the sky. A small but beautiful stitch, this image emphasises the fragility of her bond with her son and suggests that there is no longer any strong link between them; it also provides a visual reflection of her son's vulnerability and the dangers she sees in his apparent freedom.

Spasms of paper

Poppies is a poem with many semantic fields. As well as the previously explored fields of imprisonment/ liberation and textiles representing family conflict, the poem also features several references to injury and death. Opening with the ominous reminder of death through the mentions of Armistice Sunday and 'war graves', and ending in a church yard, the poem is saturated with subtle images of loss and violence, reflecting any parents' worst fears for their children. The poppy she pins to her son – already a famous symbol of loss thanks to John McCrae's poem In Flanders Field – is described as having 'crimped petals /spasms of paper red'. A powerful, emotive image that brings to mind extreme suffering, the 'spasms' suggest short bursts of severe pain [or perhaps even death throes], whilst the 'red' colouring has obvious associations with bloodshed.

Even the heavily domestic and caring imagery of the second stanza is stealthily infiltrated by the threat of violence. As previously mentioned, the choice to describe the mother's homemade Sellotape cat hair remover with the verb 'bandaged' provokes immediate associations with the treatment of injuries, perhaps comparing the mother's tender removal of cat hair with the treatment of the war injuries her son is likely to incur in the future. The innocent memory of Eskimo kisses shared 'when /you were little' is tainted by the desire to 'graze' her nose against his, once again linking to the poem's semantic field of injury. The 'gelled /blackthorns' of her son's hair, already a mournful image of the breaking down of familial bonds, has heavy religious connotations; alluding to the crucifixion of Christ, the 'blackthorns' imply that the son may be sacrificed for the greater good.

The fragility of the 'ornamental stitch' in the sky and the mother's tracing of the inscriptions of the dead leave the poem with an anxious tone of foreboding, a final image of a mother leaning against a war memorial 'like a wishbone', desperately praying for the return of her son to her safely. Though her son is still alive, she is keenly aware of his loss and mourns him – and his lost childhood – regardless.

As dismal a reading as this is, the poem can also be interpreted in a far more depressing way. As previously noted, *Poppies* is a complex poem that defies indisputable interpretation. Whilst the poem can be read as exploring a mother's sense of loss after her son grows up and goes to war, it must also be acknowledged that the poem also supports a reading where the son has died. The imagery of death could stem from the actual death of the son; the name the mother traces on the memorial could be her son's. The repeated imagery of doves, associated with peace, and birds in general can be read as symbolising the peace and freedom the son has achieved in death. In classical literature death is sometimes configured as birds taking flight; the dove's flight from the aforementioned pear tree perhaps works in this way to symbolise the loss of his life.

Regardless of the interpretation of the son's fate, *Poppies* is more than a poem about war. With its focus on emotion and loss, intertwined with the themes of memory and love, the poem develops a complex examination of the bond between mother and child and, specifically, or the emotional or psychological conflicts that can arise within this relationship.

Poppies crunched:

BEFORE - POPPIES – GRAVES – SPASMS – RED – BLOCKADE – BINDING – BANDAGED – SMOOTHED – UPTURNED – GRAZE – ESKIMOS - BLACKTHORNS – FLATTENED – DOOR – TREASURE – SPLIT – RELEASED – CAGE – SINGLE – DOVE – TUCKS – DARTS – PLEATS – TRACED – WISHBONE – FREELY – ORNAMENTAL – STITCH – PLAYGROUND – WIND

A sonnet of revision activities

1. Reverse millionaire: 10,000 points if students can guess the poem just from one word from it. You can vary the difficulty as much as you like. For example, 'clams', would be fairly easily identifiable as from Sexton's poem whereas 'fleet' would be more difficult. 1000 points if students can name the poem from a single phrase or image – 'portion out the stars and dates'. 100 points for a single line. 10 points for recognising the poem from a stanza. Play individually or in teams.

2. Research the poet. Find one sentence about them that you think sheds light on their poem in the anthology. Compare with your classmates. Or find a couple more lines or a stanza by a poet and see if others can recognise the writer from their lines.

3. Write a cento based on one or more of the poems. A cento is a poem constructed from lines from other poems. Difficult, creative, but also fun, perhaps.

4. Read 3 or 4 other poems by one of the poets. Write a pastiche. See if classmates can recognise the poet you're imitating.

5. Write the introduction for a critical guide on the poems aimed at next year's yr. 10 class.

6. Use the poet Glynn Maxwell's typology of poems to arrange the poems into different groups. In his excellent book, *On Poetry*, Maxwell suggests poems have four dominant aspects, which he calls solar,

lunar, musical and visual. A solar poem hits home, is immediately striking. A lunar poem, by contrast, is more mysterious and might not give up its meanings so easily. Ideally a lunar poem will haunt your imagination. Written mainly for the ear, a musical poem focuses on the sounds of language, rather than the meanings. Think of Lewis Carroll's *Jabberwocky*. A visual poem is self-conscious about how it looks to the eye. Concrete poems are the ultimate visual poems. According to Maxwell, the very best poems are strong in each dimension. Try applying this test to each poem. Which ones come out on top?

7. Maxwell also recommends conceptualising the context in which the words of the poem are created or spoken. Which poems would suit being read around a camp fire? Which would be better declaimed from the top of a tall building? Which might you imagine on a stage? Which ones are more like conversation overheard? Which are the easiest and which the most difficult to place?

8. Mr Maxwell is a fund of interesting ideas. He suggests all poems dramatise a battle between the forces of whiteness and blackness, nothingness and somethingness, sound and silence, life and death. In each poem, what is the dynamic between whiteness and blackness? Which appears to have the upper hand?

9. Still thinking in terms of evaluation, consider the winnowing effect of time. Which of the modern poems in the anthology do you think might be still read in 20, a 100 or 200 years? Why?

10. Give yourself only the first and last line of one of the poems. Without

peeking at the original, try to fill in the middle. Easy level: write in prose. Expert level: attempt verse.

11. According to Russian Formalist critics, poetry performs a 'controlled explosion on ordinary language'. What evidence can you find in this selection of controlled linguistic detonations?

12. A famous musician once said that though he wasn't the best at playing all the notes, nobody played the silences better. In Japanese garden water features the sound of a water drop is designed to make us notice the silence around it. Try reading one of the poems in the light of these comments, focusing on the use of white space, caesuras, punctuation – all the devices that create the silence on which the noise of the poem rests.

13. In *Notes on the Art of Poetry*, Dylan Thomas wrote that 'the best craftsmanship always leaves holes and gaps in the works of the poem so that something that is not in the poem can creep, crawl, flash or thunder in'. Examine a poem in the light of this comment, looking for its holes and gaps. If you discover these, what 'creeps', 'crawls' or 'flashes' in to fill them?

14. Different types of poems conceive the purpose of poetry differently. Broadly speaking Augustan poets of the eighteenth century aimed to impress their readers with the wit of their ideas and the elegance of the expression. In contrast, Romantic poets wished to move their readers' hearts. Characteristically Victorian poets aimed to teach the readers some kind of moral principle or example. Self-involved, avant-

garde Modernists weren't overly bothered about finding, never mind pleasing, a general audience. What impact do the CCEA anthology poems seek? Do they seek to amuse, appeal to the heart, teach us something? Are they like soliloquies – the overheard inner workings of thinking – or more like speeches or mini-plays? Try placing each poem somewhere on the following continuums. Then create a few continuums of your own. As ever, comparison with your classmates will prove illuminating.

Emotional...intellectual

Feelings...ideas

Internal..external

Contemplative...rhetorical

Open...guarded

Terminology task

The following is a list of poetry terminology and short definitions of the terms. Unfortunately, cruel, malicious individuals [i.e. us] have scrambled them up. Your task is to unscramble the list, matching each term to the correct definition. Good luck!

Term	Definition
Imagery	Vowel rhyme, e.g. 'bat' and 'lag'
Metre	An implicit comparison in which one thing is said to be
Rhythm	another
Simile	Description in poetry
Metaphor	A conventional metaphor, such as a 'dove' for peace
Symbol	A metrical foot comprising an unstressed followed by a
Iambic	stressed beat
Pentameter	A line with five beats
Enjambment	Description in poetry using metaphor, simile or
Caesura	personification
Dramatic monologue	A repeated pattern of ordered sound
Figurative imagery	An explicit comparison of two things, using 'like' or 'as'
Onomatopoeia	Words, or combinations of words, whose sounds mimic
Lyric	their meaning
Adjective	Words in a line starting with the same letter or sound
Alliteration	A strong break in a line, usually signalled by punctuation
Ballad	A regular pattern of beats in each line
Sonnet	A narrative poem with an alternating four and three beat
Assonance	line
Sensory imagery	A word that describes a noun
Quatrain	A 14-line poem following several possible rhyme
Diction	schemes
Personification	When a sentence steps over the end of a line and
	continues into the next line or stanza
	Description that uses the senses
	A four-line stanza
	Inanimate objects given human characteristics
	A poem written in the voice of a character
	A poem written in the first person, focusing on the
	emotional experience of the narrator
	A term to describe the vocabulary used in a poem.

GLOSSARY

ALLITERATION – the repetition of consonants at the start of neighbouring words in a line

ANAPAEST - a three beat pattern of syllables, unstress, unstress, stress. E.g. 'on the moon', 'to the coast', 'anapaest'

ANTITHESIS - the use of balanced opposites

APOSTROPHE – a figure of speech addressing a person, object or idea

ASSONANCE – vowel rhyme, e.g. sod and block

BLANK VERSE – unrhymed lines of iambic pentameter

BLAZON – a male lover describing the parts of his beloved

CADENCE – the rise of fall of sounds in a line of poetry

CAESURA – a distinct break in a poetic line, usually marked by punctuation

COMPLAINT – a type of love poem concerned with loss and mourning

CONCEIT – an extended metaphor

CONSONANCE – rhyme based on consonants only, e.g. book and back

COUPLET – a two-line stanza, conventionally rhyming

DACTYL – the reverse pattern to the anapaest; stress, unstress, unstress. E.g. 'Strong as a'

DRAMATIC MONOLOGUE – a poem written in the voice of a distinct character

ELEGY – a poem in mourning for someone dead

END-RHYME – rhyming words at the end of a line

END-STOPPED – the opposite of enjambment; i.e. when the sentence and the poetic line stop at the same point

ENJAMBMENT – where sentences run over the end of lines and stanzas

FIGURATIVE LANGUAGE – language that is not literal, but employs figures of speech, such as metaphor, simile and personification

FEMININE RHYME – a rhyme that ends with an unstressed syllable or unstressed syllables.

FREE VERSE – poetry without metre or a regular, set form

GOTHIC – a style of literature characterised by psychological horror, dark deeds and uncanny events

HEROIC COUPLETS – pairs of rhymed lines in iambic pentameter

HYPERBOLE – extreme exaggeration

IAMBIC – a metrical pattern of a weak followed by a strong stress, ti-TUM, like a heart beat

IMAGERY – the umbrella term for description in poetry. Sensory imagery refers to descriptions that appeal to sight, sound and so forth; figurative imagery refers to the use of devices such as metaphor, simile and personification

JUXTAPOSITION – two things placed together to create a strong contrast

LYRIC – an emotional, personal poem usually with a first-person speaker

MASCULINE RHYME – an end rhyme on a strong syllable

METAPHOR – an implicit comparison in which one thing is said to be another

METAPHYSICAL – a type of poetry characterised by wit and extended metaphors

METRE – the regular pattern organising sound and rhythm in a poem

MOTIF – a repeated image or pattern of language, often carrying thematic significance

OCTET OR OCTAVE – the opening eight lines of a sonnet

ONOMATOPOEIA – bang, crash, wallop

PENTAMETER – a poetic line consisting of five beats

PERSONIFICATION – giving human characteristics to inanimate things

PLOSIVE – a type of alliteration using 'p' and 'b' sounds

QUATRAIN – a four-line stanza

REFRAIN – a line or lines repeated like a chorus

ROMANTIC – A type of poetry characterised by a love of nature, by strong emotion and heightened tone

SESTET – the last six lines in a sonnet

SIMILE – an explicit comparison of two different things

SONNET – a form of poetry with fourteen lines and a variety of possible set rhyme patterns

SPONDEE – two strong stresses together in a line of poetry

STANZA – the technical name for a verse

SYMBOL – something that stands in for something else. Often a concrete representation of an idea.

SYNTAX – the word order in a sentence. doesn't Without sense English syntax make. Syntax is crucial to sense: For example, though it uses all the same words, 'the man eats the fish' is not the same as 'the fish eats the man'

TERCET – a three-line stanza

TETRAMETER – a line of poetry consisting of four beats

TROCHEE – the opposite of an iamb; stress, unstress, strong, weak.

VILLANELLE – a complex interlocking verse form in which lines are recycled

VOLTA – the 'turn' in a sonnet from the octave to the sestet

Recommended reading

Atherton, C. & Green, A. *Teaching English Literature 16-19*. NATE, 2013

Bate, J. Ted Hughes, *The Unauthorised Life. William Collins*, 2016

Bowen et al. *The Art of Poetry, vol.1 - 16*. Peripeteia Press, 2015-18

Brinton, I. *Contemporary Poetry*. CUP, 2009

Eagleton, T. *How to Read a Poem*. Wiley & Sons, 2006

Fry, S. *The Ode Less Travelled*. Arrow, 2007

Hamilton, I. & Noel-Todd, J. *Oxford Companion to Modern Poetry*, OUP, 2014

Heaney, S. *The Government of the Tongue*. Farrar, Straus & Giroux, 1976

Herbert, W. & Hollis, M. *Strong Words*. Bloodaxe, 2000

Howarth, P. *The Cambridge Introduction to Modernist Poetry*. CUP, 2012

Hurley, M. & O'Neill, M. *Poetic Form, An Introduction*. CUP, 2012

Meally, M. & Bowen, N. *The Art of Writing English Literature Essays*, Peripeteia Press, 2014

Maxwell, G. *On Poetry*. Oberon Masters, 2012

Padel, R. *52 Ways of Looking at a Poem*. Vintage, 2004

Padel, R. *The Poem and the Journey*. Vintage, 2008

Paulin, T. *The Secret Life of Poems*. Faber & Faber, 2011

Schmidt, M. *Lives of the Poets*. Orion, 1998

Wolosky, S. *The Art of Poetry: How to Read a Poem*. OUP, 2008.

About the author

Head of English and freelance writer, Neil Bowen has a Masters Degree in Literature & Education from Cambridge University and is a member of Ofqual's experts panel for English. He is the author of *The Art of Writing English Essays for GCSE*, co-author of *The Art of Writing English Essays for A-level and Beyond* and of *The Art of Poetry*, volumes 1-17. Neil runs the peripeteia project, bridging the gap between A-level and degree level English courses: www.peripeteia.webs.com.

Printed in Great Britain
by Amazon

36428369R00113